Reappraising Legal, Political and Ethical Questions Concerning the Herero and Nama Genocide

International Studies on Military Ethics

THE SERIES IS EDITED UNDER THE AUSPICES OF THE INTERNATIONAL SOCIETY FOR MILITARY ETHICS IN EUROPE (EUROISME)

VOLUME 13

EURO ISME
International Society for Military Ethics in Europe

The titles published in this series are listed at *brill.com/isme*

Reappraising Legal, Political and Ethical Questions Concerning the Herero and Nama Genocide

By

Julia Böcker

Translated by

Emmanuel Valentine and Sean O'Byrne

BRILL | NIJHOFF

LEIDEN | BOSTON

Library of Congress Cataloging-in-Publication Data

Names: Böcker, Julia (Julia Franziska Maria), author. | Valentine, Emmanuel, translator. | O'Byrne, Sean (Translator), translator.
Title: Reappraising legal, political, and ethical questions concerning the Herero and Nama genocide / by Julia Böcker ; translated by Emmanuel Valentine and Sean O'Byrne.
Description: Leiden ; Boston : Brill/Njhoff, 2024. | Series: International studies on military ethics, 2214-7926 ; volume 13 |
Identifiers: LCCN 2023059242 | ISBN 9789004688193 (hardback) | ISBN 9789004688209 (ebook)
Subjects: LCSH: Namibia–History–Herero Revolt, 1904-1907. | Namibia–History–Nama Revolt, 1904-1907. | Genocide–Law and legislation–Namibia–20th century. | Herero (African people)–History. | Nama (African people)–History. | William II, German Emperor, 1859-1941. | Apologizing–Social aspects. | Reparations for historical injustices.
Classification: LCC KZ6795.N36 B63? 2024 | DDC 968.81/02–dc23/eng/20240126
LC record available at https://lccn.loc.gov/2023059242

Typeface for the Latin, Greek, and Cyrillic scripts: "Brill". See and download: brill.com/brill-typeface.

ISSN 2214-7926
ISBN 978-90-04-68819-3 (hardback)
ISBN 978-90-04-68820-9 (e-book)
DOI 10.1163/9789004688209

This book is printed on acid-free paper and produced in a sustainable manner.

The jury of EuroISME's annual prize for the best student's thesis on military ethics consists of:

1. Colonel (ret) Rev. Prof. Dr. P.J. McCormack, MBE, (chairman, United Kingdom)
2. Brig.Gen. (ret) Benoît Royal (France)
3. Dr. Veronika Bock (Germany)
4. MMag. Stefan Gugerel (Austria)
5. [vacancy]
6. Dr. Asta Maskaliūnaitė (Estonia)
7. Prof.Dr. Desiree Verweij (The Netherlands)
8. Ms. Ivana Gošić (Serbia, secretary)

Triggered by protests of police violence against black people in the USA, a debate has begun in Germany about the colonial past. Will the Berlin subway station "Mohrenstraße" really be renamed "Anton-Wilhelm-Amo-Straße" after the first well-known philosopher and legal scholar of African origin in Germany? The false myth of the short, unencumbered colonial period has long persisted in this country. Debates about street names and monuments, remains in the university collections and looted property in museums give rise to hope that an awareness of colonial injustice and colonial violence is gradually growing.

This shows movement in the right direction, that Germany is facing up to its whole violent past. Further steps are still pending. In Namibia, descendants of the victims are still suffering from the aftermath of the first genocide in the 20th century. The German Empire not only had thousands of Herero and Nama disenfranchised and carried out, but also enslaved and murdered. Germany has admitted its historical guilt for the Holocaust and World War II. But it is also important to take responsibility for colonial violence.

A reappraisal includes various, highly complex aspects from historical contexts through legal channels to political means and, at best, solutions based on peace ethics. The present work provides such an established example of colonial historical work from an interdisciplinary perspective.

This thesis has been awarded the first prize of the year 2020 in EuroISME's annual contest for the best student's thesis (Master of Arts). In 2022, the thesis has received an update. For information about the contest, please visit <www.euroisme.eu>

Contents

Preface IX
Acknowledgements XII
List of Maps XIII

1 Introduction 1
1 Starting Position: Diagnosing the Problem 1
2 Enquiry/Key Questions, Aims, Research Hypotheses 2
3 Methodical Approach and Structure of This Paper 3
4 Sources and Current State of Literature and Research 4
5 Political and Scientific Relevance of This Paper 5

2 Historical Background
Genocide in the Colony 9
1 Colonial Rule in German South West Africa 9
2 Eroding the Limits of Violence in War (1904 to 1908) 12
3 Concentration Camps and Forced Labour 16
4 Consequences in the Present 18

3 On Legal Reappraisal
Category Genocide 20
1 A Crime against Human Rights? 20
2 Answers Derived from Genocide Research 25
3 Judicial Reappraisal of the Colonial Injustice 29

4 Approaches of Political Reappraisal 34
1 Forgetting, Suppressing, Avoiding 34
2 Development Aid as Compensation? 37
3 The 'G-Word' and Breaking Taboos 39
4 Politicising Colonial Injustice 41
5 German-Namibian Talks 43

5 An Ethical and Moral Approach
The Way of Apology 46
1 Requirements of a Political Apology 46
2 2004 Memorial Ceremony on the Waterberg – 'Forgive Us Our Trespasses' 48
3 Non-political Apologies 51

4 Impetus from Political Actors 52
5 Prospects of a Plea for Forgiveness 54

Conclusion 58
1 Summary 58
2 Policy Recommendation 59
3 Other Means of Reappraisal 61
4 Outlook 64

Afterword 65

Appendix 71
Sources and Literature 87

Preface

The roads and detours taken to address colonial injustice concerning the genocide of the Herero and Nama are still highly topical issues. Today's Namibia was occupied by German troops in the imperial period of the late 19th century and administered as the colony of "German South West Africa". The German Empire appropriated the people's land and livestock, stripping them of their economic livelihood and their rights. Particularly during the German-Herero War (1904–1908), men, women and children were persecuted and killed. There is also historical evidence of forced labour, concentration camps, rape and human experimentation. Genocide was committed against the Herero and Nama – the descendants of the victims suffer from the consequences to this day. Critical discussion of this part of its history was long avoided in German politics, and the term genocide remained taboo. For some time now, though, efforts have been made towards reconciliation.

Political efforts to confront the past have had impetus from numerous sources. Legal actions by those affected had, albeit unsuccessfully, repeatedly put recognition of the genocide and corresponding compensation on the agenda. The 2004 centenary of the Battle of Waterberg broke the taboo. The 100th anniversary of the Armenian genocide, which was recognised by some nations (including Germany) in 2015/2016, brought historical-political movement for acknowledging the genocide of the Herero and Nama. Since 2015, it has been a principle of German politics to speak of the grave guilt of the German state and the German colonial troops, of the war of extermination, war crimes and genocide. This has also established Germany's responsibility for the future of Namibia. To approach dealing with their common history, a German-Namibian dialogue process was started in the same year – both governments sent delegations.

This paper was awarded the prize for best Master's thesis in military ethics by the International Society for Military Ethics in Europe (EuroISME) in 2020. It is published here in its original form. Although it depicts a point somewhat in the past in the long, complex process of reappraisal, it has lost none of its relevance. It also highlights important aspects from different perspectives beyond the limits of the case study. The benefit lies in the intensive examination of complex questions of how to confront history, questions which will continue to arise in future. Politics and society have meanwhile moved further along their path. An afterword to the publication highlights the most important changes since the work was completed.

This paper argues that, in the face of the extreme violence of genocide, a political apology could be an effective instrument of conflict transformation, even when the injustice occurred well in the past. This is the case when the plea for forgiveness is bound up with other efforts. This conclusion follows from an interdisciplinary approach that examines the historical foundations, the legal approaches, the political responses and finally the ethical issues and the possibilities for peace. In coming to terms with massive systemic injustice, not only legal questions, but also peace policy and ethical considerations are relevant.

At the forefront, the relevance of historical examination of the violent past as well as efforts towards reparation must be emphasised. It is more than regrettable that other issues currently command all the political attention. In view of Russia's war of aggression against Ukraine in violation of international law, the important and urgent task of the former colonial states to find an appropriate way of addressing the violent past jointly with the descendants of the victims is at risk of being forgotten. Yet the issue is of great political and social importance on numerous levels.

The protests in the USA over violence exercised by white police officers against Black people have also triggered a long overdue confrontation with colonialism and racism in Germany. Black people and minorities of other ethnicities bring their experiences of fleeing, war and discrimination into German society. The return of looted artefacts, art objects and human remains is already sending important signals. The fact that the relationship between colonialism and the Holocaust is currently being discussed in the culture of remembrance, despite all the difficulties, also signifies interest and development. Political and social awareness of the colonial past has begun on various levels.

There is also a foreign policy dimension for Germany. The German colonial empire encompassed parts of the present-day nations of Burundi, Rwanda, Tanzania, Namibia, Cameroon, Gabon, Republic of Congo, Central African Republic, Chad, Nigeria, Togo and Ghana, the People's Republic of China as well as Papua New Guinea and several islands in the Western Pacific and Micronesia. Recognition and atonement for colonisation, exploitation and persecution have yet to be made for these territories as well.

A plea for forgiveness would also send out a European political signal. The former colonial powers are only just beginning to address the issue, while their former occupied territories are still feeling the after-effects. Britain acknowledged to Kenya in 2015 that crimes were committed on behalf of the state in the suppression of the Mau Mau guerrilla army (1952–1960). Victims won direct compensation. In Nairobi, a memorial was erected and historical archives were opened for research purposes. However, the discussions only reached a wider public in 2020, when the monument to a former slaveholder was toppled into Bristol Harbour during the "Black Lives Matter" demonstrations.

In France, too, debates about history were bound up with present-day issues, in this case: the division into left-wing and (extreme) right-wing parties. In 2017, President Emmanuel Macron addressed the decades-long denial of the Algerian war (1954–1962) and in 2020 commissioned a historical assessment. In other European countries, such as the Netherlands or Belgium, discussions on colonial army violence are now also being held, but are far from being concluded. Reflections on Germany's colonial past thus fit into a broader overall picture.

Ultimately, rapprochement between the Global North and South is essential to the international objective of halting climate change. Countries of the Global South have contributed very little to global warming, but are suffering the most from it. In Namibia, for example, the severe droughts of recent years can be attributed to climate change. Climatic extremes such as drought or flooding, with their ensuing consequences, will increase the threats and risks confronting in particular fragile regions of the globe. Past harms and taboos must be urgently addressed in order to meet the global collective challenge of delaying and adapting to climate change. In this, past and future are inextricably bound.

Hamburg, October, 2022

The colonial discourse during the time of the German Empire was on one hand determined by pejorative attributions of others (*i.e.* 'Kaffirs', 'Hottentots'), on the other by euphemistic descriptions ('protection zone', 'protective troops'). These expressions reflect incredible racism and contempt for humanity. Thus, where contemporary terms are quoted, it is exclusively for the purpose of exposing the mentality and real power structures of the time. Quotation marks indicate particularly problematic terms. Further, it is important to avoid stereotypes. At no time were the Herero and Nama people passive victims but maintained territory and dignity; nor should any other parties be regarded simplistically.[1]

To keep this paper as stringent as possible only the appendix contains the transcribed interview, maps of Namibia, primary source and biographical information about the actors.

1 See Jürgen Zimmerer, 'Krieg, KZ und Völkermord in Südwestafrika' in Jürgen Zimmerer and Joachim Zeller (Hg), *Völkermord in Deutsch-Südwestafrika: Der Kolonialkrieg (1904–1908) in Namibia und seine Folgen* (3rd edn, BPB 2016) 48.

Acknowledgements

For the supervision of the MA dissertation presented here and the warm welcome at the Center for Ethical Education in the Armed Forces (zebis), I thank Dr Veronika Bock with all my heart.

I am particularly grateful to Prof Dr Anna Geis of the Helmut Schmidt University Hamburg for kindly accepting to be a second supervisor.

I would like to give my heartfelt thanks to Prof Dr Ursula Schröder, Prof Dr Götz Neuneck, Dr Patricia Schneider and Naida Mehmedbegowić-Dreilich of the Institute for Peace Research and Security Policy (IFSH) for all their efforts in the coordination of the work.

Particular thanks to Ruprecht Polenz for his time and his openness in an amazingly exciting discussion.

I owe this to the help of Prof Dr Heinz-Gerhard Justenhoven, Institute of Theology and Peace, Hamburg, to whom I am also very grateful.

I thank Catharina Winzer, manager of the photographic archive in the Museum am Rothenbaum, Hamburg for her kind help by researching the pictures.

Many thanks to Heinrich Dierkes, Rüdiger Frank, Jan-Peter Gülden, Bianca Rossini, Maria Störch and Kristina Tonn for their collegial support at zebis.

Many times my friends Ulrike Dimitz, Thorsten Ehrbeck, Hannah Habertag, Kerstin Lohr, Bastian Roos and Johanna Willner were of great help – thank you.

The same goes for my sisters Anna-Magdalena Wachter, Daphne Böcker and Noemi Böcker, whom I also wish to thank from the bottom of my heart.

Without the enormous support of my parents, Andrea and Felix Böcker, I could not have written this paper.

I also want to thank Vincent, Julius and Catharina Böcker, my children, who were the only way I was able to take a break and think about anything else.

Above all, however, it was made possible by my husband, Patrick Böcker, his constant assurance and support and whom I wish to thank very, very much.

Maps

1 War zone in German South West Africa 80
2 Labour camps in the colony of German South West Africa 81

Alexander von Hirschfeld, Photograph, Namibia; date unknown (approximately 1905 to 1907)
SOURCE: FROM THE COLLECTION OF PHOTOGRAPHS OF THE MUSEUM AM ROTHENBAUM. *KUNST UND KULTUREN DER WELT* HAMBURG (MARKK), INV. NO. 2018.1, 85

CHAPTER 1

Introduction

A unit of soldiers marches through hilly terrain, clouded in dust. Carrying guns and baggage they traverse the undergrowth over stony ground, heading towards some buildings in the distance. Scattered horsemen accompany them. This paper is headed by a photograph, shot between 1905 and 1907 by a German lieutenant, in a country now known as Namibia. This area was declared a colony of the German Empire and the colonial army moved against the indigenous Herero and Nama people with extreme violence. The photographer selected an interesting focal point, standing behind the soldiers as if providing cover. Perspectives of the colonial war: If we consider the classification, definition and recognition of violence in Germany, then this picture will convey the subject of this paper.

1 Starting Position: Diagnosing the Problem

Germany's dealings with its colonial past are fraught with tensions. War conduct was discussed by a political committee as early as 1904. The conservative Member of Parliament, Ludwig von Reventlow, demanded in the Berlin Parliament, 'Do not use more humanity than necessary when dealing with bloodthirsty beasts in the shape of man!'[2] Such a racist and aggressive tone would seem completely incompatible with today's constitutional political values of conforming to human rights. Yet when the colonial injustices were discussed in July 2015 during a federal press conference, the classification as genocide – itself ground-breaking – only came to pass with very moderate enthusiasm.[3] Confronting the politics of the past carries a great burden.

2 Stenographic reports of the negotiations in the Reichstag (Parliament), 17 March 1904, XI election period, LX Session, vol 199, 1903/05, 1900/C, Ludwig zu Reventlow; he belonged to the racist German Social Party.

3 Source: Martin Schäfer, Speaker of the Foreign Office, 'Kolonialkrieg des Deutschen Reichs in Namibia' government press conference (Berlin, 10 July 2015) <https://www.bundesregierung.de/breg-de/aktuelles/pressekonferenzen/regierungspressekonferenz-vom-10-juli-847582>.

© EURO-ISME, 2024 | DOI:10.1163/9789004688209_002

Germany has faced reappraisal of its difficult past many times.[4] Such steps, undertaken by democratically thinking societies, committed to human rights, to cope with a past laden with dictatorship and crime, initially referred mainly to the legal, political, scientific and social process of coming to terms with the past of National Socialism (NS) as a basis for peace in Europe.[5] Questions of globalised togetherness determine our present. Therefore, the unjust, brutal colonial history, which has for centuries connected the North and the South, needs to be now at last added to the agenda.[6] However, this raises difficult, complex questions about our historical memory, judicial integration and political behaviour. Also, the difficult topic of reparation – the long-standing demand of the victims' descendants – should be considered here.[7] This too is connected with a painful process of negotiation.[8]

2 Enquiry/Key Questions, Aims, Research Hypotheses

This thesis addresses the complex question of the extent to which the brutal, deadly violence of German troops in the war against the Herero and Nama from 1904 to 1908 has become the subject of steps through which Germany is confronting its past. It is a precondition and basic understanding that history as such cannot be mastered or concluded, but that remembering and reappraisal will always remain the tasks at hand.

4 See Christoph Daase, Stefan Engert and Judith Renner, 'Guilt, Apology and Reconciliation in International Relations' in: Christopher Daase and Stefan Engert (eds), *Apology and Reconciliation in International Relations: The Importance of Being Sorry* (Routledge 2016) 15.

5 Some questions of reappraising the past are answered by Helmut König, 'Von der Diktatur zur Demokratie oder Was ist Vergangenheitsbewältigung', in: Helmut König, Michael Kohlstruck und Andreas Wöll (eds), *Vergangenheitsbewältigung am Ende des zwanzigsten Jahrhunderts* (Westdeutscher Verlag 1998) 371.

6 Hans Dieter Heimendahl, 'Wir brauchen eine neue Erinnerungskultur', *Deutschlandfunk Kultur* (Berlin, 31 January 2019).

7 See Hans Günther Hockerts, 'Wiedergutmachung in Deutschland 1945–1990. Ein Überblick' (2013) 25–26 *Aus Politik und Zeitgeschichte* 15. Like no other, the specific German term "Wiedergutmachung" contains a combination of compensation, reversal of judicial wrongdoing and other projections, but also the danger of trivialisation.

8 See Tobias Winstel, 'Vergangenheit verjährt nicht. Über Wiedergutmachung' (2013) 25–26 *Aus Politik und Zeitgeschichte* 4. On a wider context of reconciliation also Thomas Hoppe, 'Authentische Erinnerung – Fundament für tragfähige Versöhnung' in Zentralkomitee der deutschen Katholiken (ed), *Wege zur Versöhnung. Grundlagen für ein tragfähiges Miteinander* (Renovabis 2018) 82.

This forms an arc from the past across the present to the future. The historical, legal, political, ethical and social dimensions of what has been attempted, failed or is possible in the process of confronting the past are examined. Such questions regarding the use of violence by a national army also touch upon an ethical level. The question of the treatment of massive systemic injustice in (post-) conflict societies is equally important for peace and security policies as well as for peace and military ethics considerations.

Central guiding questions emerge about the actual historical events, their legal classification and how to deal with them politically.

One task is indicated by the problematic nature of our reckoning with the past so far. Only recently, the Namibian ambassador in Germany repeated his request for 'reconciliation based on respect'.[9] This implies that the approaches taken so far have been deficient. The aim is to strengthen an ethical-moral approach: the way to a political apology. So far there has been no direct recognition of the genocide by a head of state or head of government. Therefore, the aim is to clarify how Germany can make a politically effective and future-oriented apology.

3 Methodical Approach and Structure of This Paper

To reflect on such a complex and many-layered subject, various disciplines must be methodically approached. An overview of the causes, course and consequences of the war in the colony of German South West Africa begins with an historical introduction to the past that is dealt with here: Knowledge of the German colonies has been marginalised for so long, it is barely part of common teaching material. This work is based on critically analysed, interpreted sources.

The treatment of the first genocide of the 20th century is decisively determined by the debate about its (non)classification into this category. Therefore, the following chapter will concentrate on the concept shaped according to international law, but also historically and sociologically, of the difficult investigation into judicial reappraisal. The application of international legal provisions prevails here, however, since the concept is also an item of genocide research, there is an added historical, political, sociological aspect. For this, the widely recognised catalogue of criteria by social scientist Helen Fine is consulted.

---

9 Hans Jessen, 'Namibia wartet. Interview mit Andreas Guibeb' (2019), 5 *Politik und Kultur* 4.

These historical and legal foundations are necessary to subsequently explain the strategies of the political response. To this end, the behavioural patterns are brought into focus through political statements and political action. Were there reasons for attitudes and/or movements in all this? Both chapters need to show whether the individual steps, either legal evaluations or political approaches, are problematic. This is approached critically and reflectively.

If in this process the need for an alternative process becomes clear, the question arises of how such a change in direction will work: What does a political decision consist of? What work has already been done? What is still to be done? The task of this chapter is to research an ethical-moral approach for coming to terms with colonial wrongdoings. To do this, reference will be made at certain points back to the theories of political apologies, in particular the concept from political scientist Stefan Engert of public apology is applied. His list of criteria reveals the large potential but also the pitfalls of a political apology.[10]

4 Sources and Current State of Literature and Research

On account of the diversity of methods, the sources must also be chosen from a wide spectrum:

- The historical can be illuminated by documents of various provenances. If national sources (staff reports, orders, and summonses) are the official account of the belligerent powers, memoirs reveal the insider's view. It is more difficult to find evidence of the voices of the Herero and Nama, but they can be traced in missionaries' memoirs.
- Regarding international law, the relevant legal standards are consulted.
- The political discourse is examined through applications to and plenary reports from the Parliament of the Federal Republic of Germany (Bundestag) and speeches on various occasions. Furthermore, Ruprecht Polenz (CDU, Christian democratic and liberal conservative party in Germany), the German Special Envoy for the talks with Namibia was asked for an interview which can be found in its entirety in the appendix. This conversation is the most important resource for the ethical-moral approach.
- Finally, the national press reports from Germany and Namibia are important sources of information.[11]

10 See Stefan Engert, 'Die Staatenwelt nach Canossa. Eine liberale Theorie politischer Entschuldigungen' (2011) 86 (1/2) *Die Friedens-Warte* 155.

11 The *Allgemeine Zeitung* is published in one of the national languages of Namibia – German – and its content too is aimed at German-Namibians. *The Namibian* is published in English, the official language.

The academic discourse on this topic is also diverse:

- The historical reappraisal was started in both German states (Drechsler in the GDR, Bley in the BRD). Once resumed in 1990, the debate, influenced by genocide research, concentrated strongly on the question of genocide (Lau). The *Post-Colonial Turn* allowed for the viewpoint of the African population to a larger degree (Krüger). There were also approaches from global history (Zimmerer), military history (Kuß) and non-German scholars (Dedering).
- There are general legal interpretations regarding genocide in international law (Schabas). The question of whether the case of the Herero and Nama counts as a crime against international law has been differently evaluated by various authors (Kämmerer/Föh, Sarkin). Also, the law as a means for reparation is assessed (Heinemann).
- Research from political science is consulted which analyses German-Namibian relations and critically scrutinises the treatment of colonial violence (Kößler/Melber). Furthermore, the German Namibia policy is analysed in the light of interests and values (Roos/Seidl). A comparison of various historical-political commemoration discourses is also provided (Robel).
- There is a scientific discourse on political apologies that runs between political science, law, philosophy, psychology and linguistics as the disciplines addressed by the complex phenomenon (Engert, Binder, Löwenheim, Nobles amongst others). In doing so, theoretical and empirical knowledge complement each other to form a practice of apology which is analysed as a phenomenon in its own right.
- Finally the subject belongs to the wide field of reconciliation (e.g. Hoppe).

Authors of different backgrounds see in their historical inheritance a political responsibility (Kößler/Melber, Engert) and engage firmly with it (Zimmerer). This paper can build on these representations and complement them with the decidedly interdisciplinary approach of *Peace and Security Studies*.

5 Political and Scientific Relevance of This Paper

In its agreement, the grand coalition currently in government in Germany has declared a critical reappraisal of its colonial history to be one of its targets.[12]

12 See 'A new Awakening for Europe. A new Dynamic for Germany. A new Solidarity for our Country', coalition agreement of CDU, CSU and SPD for the 19th election period of the German Federal Parliament (Bundestag) (Berlin, 12 March 2018)

However, in practice this claim has not (yet) been fulfilled. Yet Germany seems, both politically and societally, to be awakening from its long-prevailing 'colonial amnesia'.[13] Changes, which in the course of this paper will be highlighted, suggest, that a 'colonial aphasia'[14] is currently being overcome. Current talks between Germany and Namibia about the colonial past give rise to hope. A plea for German government representatives to use the historical occasion to apologise to descendants of victims would therefore come just at the right time.

If the Federal Government assumes responsibility in this way, it will do justice to its own claim and to Germany's international reputation in matters of historical reappraisal.[15] Furthermore, reappraising its own violent history can make a statement about the validity of the human rights standards today. In addition, official recognition would protect it against criticism of its own country when pointing out grievances elsewhere. Instead, new relationships with former colonies can be established.

Politically this is highly topical, as Germany must position itself in its Africa policy. Many problems of today, which far exceed migration issues, have their roots in the colonial heritage. For the victimised societies this is not history. Therefore, an apologist image of European colonial forces, attributing a civilising affect to their rule, as spread in 2018 by the German chancellor's envoy for Africa, is not conducive for the future.[16] Global historians and researchers of African studies criticised it very strongly.[17] This connects a political dimension very closely with an academic focus on the matter.

In scientific terms, this paper inhabits an interesting junction between historical culture, international human rights law and Africa policy. Colonial

---

<https://www.bundesregierung.de/breg-de/themen/koalitionsvertrag-zwischen-cdu-csu-und-spd-195906>, 154 on cultural cooperation with Africa; 167, 169 on remembrance and commemoration.

13 See Stuart Hall, *Ideologie, Identität, Repräsentation*. Ausgewählte Schriften 4 (Argument Verlag 2004) 199; Jürgen Zimmerer, *Von Windhuk nach Auschwitz? Beiträge zum Verhältnis von Kolonialismus und Holocaust* (LIT-Verlag 2011), 14, 44. The current awakening is also recognized by Christine Habermalz, 'Zaghafte Aufarbeitung nach langer Amnesie' in: *Deutschlandfunk* (Cologne, 5 June 2018).

14 Ann Laura Stoler, 'Colonial Aphasia: Race and Disabled Histories in France' (2011) 23 (1) *Public History* 121. Aphasia is a psychological speech disorder or inability to find words.

15 See Stefan Engert, 'Germany – Namibia. The Belated Apology to the Herero', in: Christopher Daase and Stefan Engert (eds), *Apology and Reconciliation in International Relations: The Importance of Being Sorry* (Routledge 2016), 141.

16 See Ulrike Ruppel, 'Wir haben lange Zeit zu viel im Hilfsmodus gedacht. Interview mit Günter Nooke (CDU)' *Berliner Zeitung* (Berlin, 6 October 2018).

17 Interview with Jürgen Zimmerer, 'Afrika-Beauftragter nicht mehr tragbar!', *Westdeutscher Rundfunk* (Cologne, 9 October 2018); on the review also Anna Reuß, 'Archaische Ansichten', *Süddeutsche Zeitung* (Munich, 8 March 2019) 15.

violence – long marginalised in the collective memory[18] – has since 1990 again been a topic in Germany. The rise of memory research, the debate about continuities between 20th century conflicts, emerging genocide research and the influence of *Postcolonial Studies* can be credited with this.[19] Its beginnings can be seen for instance in exhibitions, media reports and last, but not least, satirical contributions.[20] But while Germany is just becoming conscious of this past,[21] in Namibia the consequences of the violent excesses are very much present today and constitute a great burden for descendants of the victims.[22]

Was international law useful as a means of post-conflict resolution? Was compensation important for German policy? What has been gained by the current negotiations? This paper deals with complex questions of addressing violent pasts for peace and conflict research. As Hamburg is considered the "decisive colonial metropolis of the empire,"[23] its Institute for Peace Research and Security Policy seems well placed to present an account of how Germany dealt with this period. Processes and practises, summarised as *Transitional Justice,* i.e. legal and (social) political instruments for conflict transformation, are analysed; answers to the question of how reconciliation can be achieved.[24]

---

18 "The junk room of historical memory" called it Anke Schwarzer, 'Nama und Herero. Völkermord ohne Entschädigung?' 60 *Blätter für deutsche und internationale Politik* 14.

19 See Winfried Speitkamp, 'Kolonialdenkmäler' in Jürgen Zimmerer (ed), *Kein Platz an der Sonne. Erinnerungsorte der deutschen Kolonialgeschichte* (BPB 2013) 418.

20 Examples are 'Namibia – Deutschland. Eine geteilte Geschichte'. Exhibition in the Rautenstrauch-Joest-Museum Cologne (25 November 2004 to 24 April 2005); *Hereroland. Eine deutsch-namibische Geschichte,* Thalia Theater Hamburg, world premiere on 19 January 2020 and as satirical contributions Birte Schneider and Oliver Welke, 'Genozid – Reine Ansichtssache', *Heute Show / ZDF* (Cologne, 3 June 2016) as well as Jan Böhmermann: 'Eier aus Stahl' *Neo Magazin Royal / ZDFneo* (Cologne, 14 November 2019).

21 Reflections have begun, however, it is arguable whether they are wide enough states Yvonne Robel, *'Verhandlungssache Genozid: Zur Dynamik geschichtspolitischer Deutungskämpfe* (Fink 2013) 267. A (too?) slow change is observed by John Eligon, 'Colonial Past Weighs on Germany / The Big Hole in Germany's Nazi Reckoning? Its Colonial History' *New York Times* (New York, 11 September 2018) A4.

22 See Reinhart Kößler and Henning Melber, *Völkermord – und was dann? Die Politik deutsch-namibischer Vergangenheitsbearbeitung* (Brandes & Apsel 2017) 12, 45.

23 Kilian Trotier, 'Das waren in Hamburg geplante Raubzüge', *Die Zeit* 27 June 2019, 19.

24 See Stefan Engert and Christoph Daase, 'Aufarbeitung von Schuld in den internationalen Beziehungen: Überlegungen zum „erweiterten Schuldbegriff"' in Stefan Engert and Thorsten Moos (eds), *Vom Umgang mit Schuld: Eine multidisziplinäre Annäherung* (Campus Verlag 2016) 347; Stefan Engert and Anja Jetschke, 'Transitional Justice 2.0 – Zur konzeptionellen Erweiterung eines noch jungen Forschungsprogramms' (2011) 86 (1/2) *Die Friedens-Warte* 15.

In particular, this paper offers expert knowledge relating to the potential of political apology as such a strategy and recommends a policy accordingly.

The recommendation of such a step refers to the question, 'In the face of such "unspeakable truths", would it not be better to simply, silently, bow down?'[25] In the face of unspeakable truths[26] – experiences of violence so terrible that they leave the victims speechless – a symbolic gesture on the part of the perpetrator is seen as more effective than any other conduct. We may remember the genuflection by German Chancellor Willy Brandt on 7th December 1970 in Poland at the Memorial for the dead of the Warsaw Ghetto, which was internationally understood as a plea for forgiveness for German crimes during the Second World War. Would such a gesture also be desirable in this current case? The manner of questioning would expect a positive reply. However, it is imperative to legitimise this affirmation and to bring about good reasons for a plea for forgiveness by Germany to the Herero and Nama.

---

25 See Kora Andrieu, '"Sorry for the Genocide". How Public Apologies Can Help Promote National Reconciliation' (2009) 38 (1) *Millennium: Journal of International Studies* 5.

26 See Priscilla B. Hayner, *Unspeakable Truths. Transitional Justice and the Challenge of Truth Commissions* (2nd edn, Taylor & Francis 2010) 146 with reference to the psychiatric viewpoint of Judith Lewis Herman, *Trauma and Recovery* (Pandora 2015) 1: 'Certain violations of the social compact are too terrible to utter aloud; this is the meaning of the word unspeakable'. As strong as the desire for repression, so strong too is the power of memories.

CHAPTER 2

Historical Background

Genocide in the Colony

1 Colonial Rule in German South West Africa

Pre-colonial Namibian societies today are classified as more open than the fictional European attributions as "tribes", *i.e.* supposed biological-ethnic units, would suggest.[27]

The 'golden 19th century'[28] of the Herero people was shaped by important transformations; it is not accidental that Herero means 'herders'. The fact that from 1850 they built up large cattle herds had several benefits: The animals provided the important *omaere*, soured milk, the foundation of life, secured prosperity by a trade route through to the Cape, defined status and were of cultural and sacral importance. Despite seasonal wandering, settlements were not abandoned.[29] Watering holes and cisterns were key elements of their landscape as boundary markers, which only became important with the requirements of the colonial masters.[30]

Germans appeared in the region at the beginning of the 19th century. Whalers, traders seeking natural resources and big-game hunters were the first to come into contact with the native population. Missionaries built mission stations, which also served as trading posts for consumables, guns, cattle and horses. The availability of modern weapons gave the Herero the opportunity to militarise. Through negotiating peace agreements, the missionaries also gained

27 See Gesine Krüger, 'Das Goldene Zeitalter der Viehzüchter. Namibia im 19. Jahrhundert' in Jürgen Zimmerer and Joachim Zeller (eds), *Völkermord in Deutsch-Südwestafrika: Der Kolonialkrieg (1904–1908) in Namibia und seine Folgen* (3rd edn, BPB 2016) 17; see also appended map 1, war zone in German South West Africa, 80.

28 See Dag Henrichsen, *Herrschaft und Alltag im vorkolonialen Zentralnamibia: Das Herero- und Damaraland im 19. Jahrhundert* (Basler Afrika Bibliographien 2011) XV for the history of the Herero, also known as Ovaherero.

29 For details about the Herero during the 19th century see Gesine Krüger, *Kriegsbewältigung und Geschichtsbewusstsein: Realität, Deutung und Verarbeitung des deutschen Kolonialkriegs in Namibia 1904 bis 1907* (Vandenhoeck & Ruprecht 1999) 30.

30 A typical colonial transformation into a territorial society according to Henning Melber, 'Grenzen des (post-)kolonialen Staates: Von Deutsch-Südwest nach Namibia' in Joachim Becker and Andrea Komlosy (eds), *Grenzen Weltweit. Zonen, Linien Mauern im historischen Vergleich* (2nd edn, Promedia-Verlag 2006) 129.

political power.[31] For the German occupation had been preceded by ongoing conflicts between the indigenous populations spanning several generations.[32]

Within the approximate borders between the line of Outjo to Grootfontein in the north, the Namib desert in the West, the Kalahari desert with its outlier Omaheke (Herero for Sandfeld) in the East and the area around Windhoek in the south lived 70,000 to 80,000 Herero, 30,000 to 40,000 Damara and San as well as 3,000 to 4,000 Basters; the estimates indicate in particular the population distribution. The country of Ovambo (less affected by the colonial occupation) lay at the northern border. To the south lived 15,000 to 20,000 nomadic Nama, many of whose forbears had come from the Cape colony.[33]

A tobacco merchant, Adolf Lüderitz, exploited their search for support by buying land in 1883 from the Nama *Kaptein* ("leader") Joseph Frederiks.[34] On 24th April 1884, at Lüderitz's request, Imperial Chancellor Otto von Bismarck declared the region a 'protected zone',[35] to secure it in the competition with European powers for raw materials and other key materials and also international prestige.[36]

'The Germans wanted land from Samuel Maharero. Maharero took a tin and gave them soil and he said, there is the soil you asked for'.[37] The oral record highlights the commanding behaviour of the Herero towards the arrivals. Maharero

---

31 On the mission stations as new centres of power see Krüger, 'Das Goldene Zeitalter' (n 27) 21.

32 See Dag Henrichsen, 'Die Hegemonie der Herero in Zentralnamibia zu Beginn der deutschen Kolonialherrschaft', in: Larissa Förster, Dag Henrichsen and Michael Bollig (eds), *Namibia – Deutschland. Eine geteilte Geschichte: Widerstand, Gewalt, Erinnerung* (Ed. Minerva 2004) 46.

33 Numbers for 1892 according to Theodor Leutwein, *Elf Jahre Gouverneur in Deutsch-Südwestafrika* (Mittler 1906) 11; see Jürgen Zimmerer, *Deutsche Herrschaft über Afrikaner: Staatlicher Machtanspruch und Wirklichkeit im kolonialen Namibia* (2nd edn, LIT Verlag 2002) 18.

34 Lüderitz acquired the Bay of Angra Pequena (later 'Lüderitz Bay') through a dubious agreement.

35 The term is decidedly about the protection of German interests, see Stefan Engert, 'Politische Schuld, moralische Außenpolitik? Deutschland, Namibia und der lange Schatten der kolonialen Vergangenheit', in Sebastian Harnisch, Hans W. Maull and Siegfried Schieder (eds): *Solidarität und internationale Gemeinschaftsbildung* (Campus Verlag 2009) 28.

36 See Ulrike Lindner, 'Deutscher Kolonialismus im internationalen Kontext' in Deutsches Historisches Museum (ed), *Deutscher Kolonialismus: Fragmente seiner Geschichte und Gegenwart*, (Theiss Verlag 2016) 19; see also Rainer Tetzlaff, *Afrika. Eine Einführung in Geschichte, Politik und Gesellschaft* (Springer VS 2018) 97. On 15 November 1884 Bismarck opened the Berlin Conference, to vote for the European interests.

37 See Karla Poewe, *The Namibian Herero: A History of their Psychosocial Disintegration and Survival* (Mellen Press 1985) 69 n 17, even though the paper on the psychological disease-mongering of the Herero people during the post war years has been criticised, namely from Krüger, 'Kriegsbewältigung' (n 29) 12.

styled himself as Chief, leader of a yet fictitious nation in the making.[38] But internal rivalries in the region soon worked to the advantage of the German officials by their supporting local leaders and receiving land in return.[39] The so-called "Protective Forces" carried out military actions against resisters. An administrative apparatus was established with the goal of founding a 'white' settler colony, acquiring land and cattle through unscrupulous loans, robbery or expropriation.[40]

This systematically undermined the foundations of the pastoral Herero society. Therefore, the outbreak of cattle fever of 1987 proved catastrophic.[41] Many were poverty-stricken, forced to sell massive parts of their land and to hire themselves out as cheap labour for the Germans. Pastureland was lost to a railroad line. Concerned about unrest, the colonial administration planned reserves, but was primarily focused on the interests of the settlers.[42]

The balance of power had fundamentally changed. The Herero were politically disempowered, legally discriminated against, economically dispossessed, their society profoundly disrupted. Today this is considered to be the actual cause of the war.[43]

38 See Henrichsen, *Herrschaft und Alltag* (n 28) 282; Gerhard Pool, *Samuel Maharero* (Gamsberg Macmillan Publishing 1991) 1.

39 See Reinhart Kößler and Henning Melber, 'Völkermord und Gedenken. Der Genozid an den Herero und Nama 1904–1908', in: Irmtrud Wojak, Susanne Meinl, Fritz Bauer Institut (eds), *Völkermord und Kriegsverbrechen in der ersten Hälfte des 20. Jahrhunderts* (Campus-Verlag 2004) 43; Susanne Kuß, *Deutsches Militär auf kolonialen Kriegsschauplätzen: Eskalation von Gewalt zu Beginn des 20. Jahrhunderts* (2nd edn, Links 2010) 80.

40 See Leutwein (n 33) 246; the standard works reveal backgrounds in detail, see Horst Drechsler, *Südwestafrika unter deutscher Kolonialherrschaft. Der Kampf der Herero und nama gegen den deutschen Imperialismus (1884– 1915)* (Akademie-Verlag 1966) 150 and Helmut Bley, *Kolonialherrschaft und Sozialstruktur in Deutsch-Südwestafrika 1894-1914* (Leibnitz-Verlag 1968)189.

41 In some places, 95 percent of the cattle herds died, see Jan-Bart Gewald, *Towards Redemption: A Socio-Political History of the Herero of Namibia between 1890 and 1923* (CNWS Publications 1996) 138.

42 For example, areas rich with water were cut off from it, see Krüger, *Kriegsbewältigung* (n 29) 63.

43 The process has been described as an 'erosion' by Zimmerer, 'Deutsche Herrschaft' (n 33) 27; bestätigend Susanne Kuß, 'Der Herero-Deutsche Krieg und das deutsche Militär: Kriegsursachen und Kriegsverlauf', in Larissa Förster, Dag Henrichsen and Michael Bollig (eds), *Namibia – Deutschland. Eine geteilte Geschichte: Widerstand, Gewalt, Erinnerung* (Ed. Minerva 2004), 64. A letter proves that the Herero themselves recognised this, see Krüger, *Kriegsbewältigung* (n 29) 44, 55.

2 Eroding the Limits of Violence in War (1904 to 1908)

What followed was extreme violence with complex, multi-faceted dynamics.[44] The catalyst was a sudden crisis in the south. It was the day to day business of the forces to put down such occasional rebellious flare-ups, but this left the land of Herero people unprotected. The war started on 12th January 1904; the Herero stormed farms, cut train lines and telegraph connections and occupied towns and villages.[45] There is a theory of a self-fulfilling prophecy by which the Germans, waiting for an attack by the Herero, who were not intent on war, (over)reacted.[46] This is contradicted by the fact that Chiefs had convened the year before to discuss ways out of their problem situation. This indicates a conscious decision, even if the battles did not break out at the same time, which could have been due to coordination problems.[47]

At the beginning of the war, the Herero killed more than 100 Germans, in particular (male) settlers and traders. In the words of Chief Michael Tjiseseta, 'I do not wage war on women and children, only on men!'[48] The German soldiers were aware of this strategy.[49] This supports the theory that the Herero aimed at a limited war to redress political undermining and economic dispossession. New research has found that reports and pictures of atrocities involving women as war victims were propaganda.[50]

---

44 A recent reference to the influence of emotion on extreme violence gives Matthias Häussler, *Der Genozid an den Herero: Krieg, Emotion und extreme Gewalt in „Deutsch-Südwestafrika"* (Velbrück Wissenschaft 2018) 11; see also appended map 1, war zone in German South West Africa, 80.

45 This was conveyed in a telegram to the Foreign Office in Berlin from Lieutenant Johannes Techow, Windhuk (sic), (11 January 1904), Federal Archive (Germany), location Berlin-Lichterfelde, inventory Imperial Colonial Office, Barch R 1001/2111 <https://weimar.bundesarchiv.de/DE/Content/Virtuelle-Ausstellungen/Der-Krieg-Gegen-Die-Herero-1904/der-krieg-gegen-die-herero-1904.html> 1. On the causes and phases of the war Kuß, *Deutsches Militär* (n 39) 78.

46 See Gewald, *Towards Redemption* (n 41) 178.

47 See Kuß, 'Der Herero-Deutsche Krieg' (n 43) 67.

48 This was stated by a missionary, Hanni Ziegler, 'Erinnerungen aus dem Herero-Aufstande' (1906) 42 *Daheim* 11.

49 See Kommandeur Ludwig von Estorff, *Wanderungen in Südwestafrika, Ostafrika und Südafrika 1894–1910* (Meinert 1979) 110.

50 See Gesine Krüger, 'Bestien und Opfer: Frauen im Kolonialkrieg', in Jürgen Zimmerer and Joachim Zeller (eds), *Völkermord in Deutsch-Südwestafrika: Der Kolonialkrieg (1904–1908) in Namibia und seine Folgen* (3rd edn, BPB 2016) 148. To some extent, a historical narrative accusing the Herero of great brutality has survived to the present day, perhaps as a result of this propaganda.

The Herero's war strategy and conduct corresponded to the pattern of violent conflicts in the pre-colonial era. As they did not have an army, they avoided larger battles against the German 'protective forces', carrying out guerrilla attacks and moving with their families and herds to locations where they could assemble. Yet with approximately 8000 fighters, armed with 2500 to 4000 guns, they were, at the start of the war, superior in numbers.[51]

Although the 2000 German soldiers had artillery and machines guns, at the beginning of the war they were still at a disadvantage due to the shift to the south. Initially they conceded considerable defeats. The forces were continuously enlarged by new units, but the heat, lack of water, rough terrain and typhus posed difficulties. During this first phase of the war (January to June 1904) the forces were still headed by Governor Theodor Leutwein. His warfare was limited to the goal of defeating the enemy and forcing it to surrender. Even in wartime he continued to correspond with the Herero.[52]

His leadership was deemed by the settlers too conciliatory and was harshly criticised. They saw their possessions and lives seriously threatened by the violent conflict and demanded punishment and extermination; the war should be used to give them final ownership of land and property.[53] Angry settlers and troops carried out bloody campaigns, which were classed as 'brutalisation from below'.[54]

With that grew the fear amongst the Herero of being made accountable without having been involved. 'Without doubt, the Germans will wreak terrible revenge',[55] they were told by a missionary in February, so that other Chiefs

51 Preußen Großer Generalstab, *Die Kämpfe der deutschen Truppen in Südwestafrika auf Grund amtlichen Materials bearbeitet von der Kriegsgeschichtlichen Abteilung I des Großen Generalstabs, Band 1: Der Feldzug gegen die Herero,* Mittler 1906–1908, 17. See also Kuß, *Deutsches Militär* (n 39) 82.

52 See Horst Drechsler, *Aufstände in Südwestafrika: Der Kampf der Herero und Nama 1904 bis 1907 gegen die deutsche Kolonialherrschaft* (Dietz 1984) 67 and Kuß, *Deutsches Militär* (n 39) 83.

53 See Dierk Walter, 'Kein Pardon. Zum Problem der Kapitulation im Imperialkrieg' (2012) 21 (3) *Mittelweg 36* 107.

54 See Matthias Häussler, Trutz von Trotha, 'Brutalisierung von 'unten'. Kleiner Krieg, Entgrenzung der Gewalt und Genozid im kolonialen Deutsch-Südwestafrika' (2012) 21 (3) *Mittelweg 36* 57; see also Henrik Lundtofte, '"I Believe that the Nation as such must be Annihilated". The Radicalization of the German Suppression of the Herero Rising in 1904', in Steven L. B. Jensen (ed), *Genocide: Cases, Comparisons and Contemporary Debates* (Danish Centre for Holocaust and Genocide Studies 2003), 29.

55 Missionary August Elger to the Rheinische Mission, 10 February 1904 quoted from Drechsler, *Südwestafrika unter Deutscher Kolonialherrschaft* (n 40) 169.

joined the fighting. There was dissent about how to proceed: various Chiefs were prepared to negotiate, while others dismissed it altogether.[56]

Certainly, all talks were rejected by Berlin. When the General Staff, not familiar with the terrain, took over the military leadership, it became clear that this was no longer just a case of quashing a rebellion. In differentiating from previous colonial skirmishes, one of the "points of departure"[57] towards complete escalation is found here. The change of the overall command on the ground marked the complete break with military convention, by introducing the second war phase (June to December 1904).

Lieutenant General Lothar von Trotha, infamous for his extreme militarism ('Nur-Militär'),[58] declared the *de jure* state of war and later reasoned:

> Tribes of Africa (…) are all the same in their way of thinking, they only succumb to violence. To carry out this violence with crass terrorism and even cruelty was and is my policy. I exterminate rebelling tribes with floods of blood and floods of money.[59]

In the drive for an all-embracing and decisive battle, the 'Panacea of German Warfare',[60] the Waterberg Plateau in the centre of the country was surrounded by the German forces. Approximately 60,000 Herero – men, women and children, had come together there. 6,000 were armed, but did not have artillery or much ammunition. On 11 and 12 August 1904 they were attacked by 4,000 soldiers with 36 cannons and 14 machine guns.[61]

---

56 See Zimmerer, *Deutsche Herrschaft* (n 33) 33; see also Pool (n 38) 223.

57 Zimmerer, 'Krieg, KZ und Völkermord' (n 1) 49. A "military-dominated phalanx" is recognized by Kirsten Zirkel, 'Military Power in German Colonial Policy: The Schutztruppen and Their Leaders in East and South-West Africa, 1888–1918' in David Killingray and David Omissi (eds), *Guardians of Empire: The Armed Forces of the Colonial Powers c. 1700–1964* (Manchester University Press 1999) 99.

58 Drechsler, *Aufstände in Südwestafrika* (n 52) 75. Trotha fought in German East Africa in 1896 and in China in 1900/01, and was known for his brutality.

59 Letter from General Lothar von Trotha to Gouverneur Theodor Leutwein (5 November 1904), quoted from Drechsler, *Südwestafrika unter deutscher Kolonialherrschaft* (n 40) 180. Drechsler describes von Trotha's statement as brutal and primitive.

60 See Kuß, 'Der Herero-Deutsche Krieg' (n 43) 71 with reference to this means in the later strategic-operational 'Schlieffen-Plan' on German operations and with considerations as to whether the inclusion of a natural obstacle had already been tested at the Waterberg.

61 See Preußen Großer Generalstab (n 51) 158; about the process Conrad Rust, *Krieg und Frieden im Hererolande: Aufzeichnungen aus dem Kriegsjahre 1904* (Kittler 1905) 370; see Kuß, *Deutsches Militär* (n 39) 88; about the violence Dominik J. Schaller, 'Genocide and Mass Violence in the 'Heart of Darkness': Africa in the Colonial Period', in: Donald

The songs of the women survived the battles, 'Who owns the land of the Herero? We own the land of the Herero'.[62] It is not clear, why the Herero people neither secured their position nor fled – the most likely reason is that they hoped for negotiations.[63] Their military defeat following the battle was indisputable. However, the attacks on them continued so that flight was the only way out. It is still contested whether the waterless terrain was part the German war plan or simply as advantage.[64] Whatever the case, the weakest part of their forces was stationed at this part of the siege. The comment of the General Staff was, 'The waterless Omaheke shall finish what German weapons began'.[65]

Trotha commanded that the edges of the desert be patrolled, which proved impossible due to the heat and the type of terrain. The troops then took position at the overloaded watering holes to attack those fleeing. Finally, on 2 October 1904 von Trotha issued a proclamation threatening all Herero with death, whether they had been participated in the fighting or not.[66] Prisoners-of-war were to distribute copies. All offers of negotiation or surrender were rejected. More people died at that time of thirst and exhaustion than had in the battles.[67]

During autumn of 1904 the battles moved south due to attacks by the Nama. The settlers' rigorous pursuit of their people, as well as rumours about the

---

Bloxham and A. Dirk Moses (eds), *The Oxford Handbook of Genocide Studies* (Oxford University Press 2010) 345.

62 See Wilhelm Anz, 'Gerechtigkeit für die Deutschen in Südwestafrika!' *Die christliche Welt* (Marburg, 7 July 2004) 657. See Dag Henrichsen, '„Ehi rOvaherero". Mündliche Überlieferungen von Herero zu ihrer Geschichte im vorkolonialen Namibia' (1994) 9 *WerkStatt Geschichte* 1 and Krüger, 'Bestien und Opfer' (n 50) 149 for the important supporting role of the Herero women in the war.

63 This assumes Pool (n 38) 253; agreement from Kuß, 'Der Herero-Deutsche Krieg' (n 43) 72.

64 Discussed by Walter Nuhn, *Sturm über Südwest. Der Hereroaufstand von 1904: Ein düsteres Kapitel der deutschen kolonialen Vergangenheit Namibias* (Bernard & Graefe 1989) 229; see Kuß, Deutsches Militär (n 39) 90.

65 Preußen Großer Generalstab (n 51) 207.

66 Lothar von Trotha, Proclamation to the Herero people, 2 October 1904, quoted from Michael Behnen (ed), *Quellen zur deutschen Außenpolitik im Zeitalter des Imperialismus 1890–1911* (Wissenschaftliche Buchgesellschaft 1977) 291. Transcripts can be found in the Bundesarchiv Berlin Lichterfelde and in the Militärarchiv Freiburg, a version in Otjiherero from the Botswana National Archives is found in Jan-Bart Gewald, 'The Great General of the Kaiser' (1994) 26 *Botswana Notes and Records 73*. The source is printed in the appendix to this publication on page 71. For interpretation and history, see also Kuß, *Deutsches Militär (n 39) 93*.

67 See Isabel V. Hull, *Absolute Destruction: Military Culture and the Practices of War in Imperial Germany* (Cornell University Press 2005) 44; for victim numbers see Zimmerer, *Deutsche Herrschaft* (n 33) 39.

merciless warfare against the Herero, led the Nama to enter the war. Their combat strategy of many guerrilla attacks and their familiarity with the area took advantage of the agility of their – at most – 2000 fighters. This took its toll in the Germans. Despite their radical approach, the protracted, gruelling war was a loss of face for them. Finally, the war was decided only by the tactic of imprisoning or deporting African prisoners.[68] Nevertheless the war lasted until 1908 – and there were also German losses.[69]

3 Concentration Camps and Forced Labour

In December 1904 the firing order against the Herero people was lifted. It seemed sensible to imprison those who had survived in hiding as the German troops were needed elsewhere. This heralded the final phase of the war (December 1904 to January 1908). With the aid of the mission, the prisoners of war, including women and children, were brought to camps.[70] Not only would that stop them from supporting the battles or participating in them, they could now also be exploited to build train lines, roads and piers. For the first time, the term 'Konzentrationslager' (concentration camp) was used in the German language.[71]

The prisoners were kept under atrocious conditions: They lacked food, clothing and medical care; they were inadequately protected in cramped quarters and diseases and even epidemics were rampant.[72] On top of the extreme

68 To Cameroon and Togo – 'a hugely painful Odyssey' for all involved, see Kuß, 'Deutsches Militär', 100.

69 20.876 troops were sent. 888 died in battle or through accidents, 725 died of diseases. Kommando der Schutztruppen im Reichs-Kolonialamt, Sanitätsbericht über die Kaiserliche Schutztruppe für Südwestafrika, Band 1: Administrativer Teil, Mittler 1909; 8 sowie Band 2: Statistischer Teil, Mittler 1920, 2. See also Kuß, *Deutsches Militär* (n 39) 306.

70 See Jürgen Zimmerer, 'Kriegsgefangene im Kolonialkrieg. Der Krieg gegen die Herero und Nama in Deutsch-Südwestafrika (1904–1907)' in Rüdiger Overmans (ed), *In der Hand des Feindes. Kriegsgefangenschaft von der Antike bis zum Zweiten Weltkrieg* (Böhlau Verlag 1999) 285. See also map 2, labour camps in German South West Africa, 81.

71 This term, nowadays used only for Nazi death camps, was coined in 1896 by Spanish colonialists in Cuba to describe the detention of civilians. See Joël Kotek and Pierre Rigoulot, *Das Jahrhundert der Lager: Gefangenschaft, Zwangsarbeit, Vernichtung (Propyläen 2001) 27.*

72 This was very clearly documented by missionaries' reports e.g. Heinrich Vedder, *Kurze Geschichten aus einem langen Leben* (Verlag der Rheinischen Missionsgesellschaften 1953) 135; see also Jon Bridgman and Leslie J. Worley, 'Genocide of the Hereros' in Samuel Totten, William S. Parsos and Israel W. Charny (eds), *Century of Genocide: Eyewitness Accounts and Critical Views* (Routledge 2004) 37.

physical labour, abuse was common, either whipping or sexual abuse of the women. The conditions on Shark Island and in Swakopmund were particularly frightful on account of the harsh sea climate.[73]

Until 1907 the detention camps admitted approximately 20,000 prisoners of war. Only when German settlers complained about a lack of workers did the colonial policies start to change. Von Trotha had been called back to Berlin in 1905, after the war against the Nama had failed to result in victory. But even then, the administration and military command continued the policy of detention.[74] On 31 March 1907 the war was declared over, but the internment was only lifted on 27 January 1908, the birthday of Kaiser Wilhelm II. As the camps are seen today as a continuation of the war, this date is used to mark its end.[75] Moreover, in order to properly convey the devastation, the violent conflict is no longer referred to as a "rebellion", but as a war.[76]

Until the invasion of South African military forces during the First World War, the Germans rigidly exercised control. In the face of all fantasies of world dominion, the indigenous group survived with their identities intact, and even during the period of foreign rule society began to (re)organise itself.[77] But the war had fundamentally changed the political, economic and social structures.

73 See Casper W. Erichsen, 'Zwangsarbeit im Konzentrationslager auf der Haifischinsel' in Jürgen Zimmerer and Joachim Zeller (eds), *Völkermord in Deutsch-Südwestafrika: der Kolonialkrieg (1904–1908) in Namibia und seine Folgen* (3rd edn, BPB 2016) 83.

74 See Krüger, 'Kriegsbewältigung' (n 29) 54. Only very slowly was the detention policy changed into workforce policy.

75 See Jürgen Zimmerer, 'Der erste Völkermord des 20. Jahrhunderts. Über den schwierigen Umgang mit Deutschlands kolonialem Erbe' in: Deutsches Historisches Museum (ed), *Deutscher Kolonialismus: Fragmente seiner Geschichte und Gegenwart* (Theiss Verlag 2016) 60; also Jeremy Sarkin, *Colonial Genocide and Reparations Claims in the 21st Century: The Socio-Legal Context of Claims under International Law by the Herero against Germany for Genocide in Namibia, 1904–1908* (PSI 2009) 17.

76 See Kuß, 'Der Herero-Deutsche Krieg' (n 43) 74.

77 This process, the creative *Otjiiserandu* culture of remembrance and the funeral of Chief Samuel Maharero as the initial event for development of the nation is described by Jan-Bart Gewald, 'Die Beerdigung von Samuel Maharero und die Reorganisation der Herero' in Jürgen Zimmerer and Joachim Zeller (eds), *Völkermord in Deutsch-Südwestafrika. Der Kolonialkrieg (1904–1908) und seine Folgen* (3rd edn, BPB 2016) 215.

4 Consequences in the Present

Even more than a century later the effects of the war are still felt as a 'structural, material and social-psychological legacy'[78] in Namibia. This is particularly noticeable in the distribution of land. It is a direct consequence of the colonial occupation that 70 percent of the land is still in the hands of ethnic German or foreign owners who make up five percent of the population.[79]

In general, the demographic structure of today would be different if the war had not taken place. Today, the Ovambo in the North constitute half of the approximately 2.5 million citizens.[80] The Herero, the largest group prior to the war, are now a minority of 7.5 percent with 150,000 to 200,000 people. The Nama now make up five percent alongside other small groups, based on ethnicity and linguistic affiliation. Approximately 20,000 descendants of colonialists speak German as their native tongue; overall around 100,000 Namibians are white (as of July 2018).[81] However, the data are not easy to interpret; figures are not collected for all aspects.

Namibia is economically extremely unequal. Although the general economy displays a good middle income, it suffers seriously from poverty (Gini Index: 61.0). While it occupies a middle position in the Human Development Index (HDI) (0.647), the inequalities according to the Inequality-adjusted Human Development Index (IHDI) are comparatively large (0.422) with a difference of 34.8 percent between the two indicators.[82]

The memory of the war lives on in the direct descendants of the victims and is the main reference for their identity construction. It is also about symbolic power in national memory, where the dominant narrative of the numerically superior and politically leading Ovambo was long the struggle against the

78 See Kößler and Melber, *Völkermord – Und was dann* (n 22) 12, 45; Kößler and Melber, 'Völkermord und Gedenken' (n 39) 60.

79 Data according to the Namibia Statistics Agency, 'Namibia Land Statistics Booklet' (September 2018) <https://nsa.nsa.org.na/wp-content/uploads/2021/09/Namibia_Land_Statistics_2018.pdf> 48.

80 Since they were less impacted by colonial occupation, there was no population census during this period.

81 Data from Central Intelligence Agency, 'The World Factbook' (1 November 2023) < https://www.cia.gov/the-world-factbook/countries/namibia>.

82 Data from Human Development Report of the development programme of the United Nations (UNDP), 'Human Development Index and its Components' (2019) <http://www.hdr.undp.org/en/composite/HDI> and 'Inequalities in Human Development in the 21st Century. Briefing note for countries on the 2019 Human Development Report' <http://hdr.undp.org/sites/all/themes/hdr_theme/country-notes/NAM.pdf>. For interpretation see also Reinhold Kößler, 'Namibia and Germany', *Negotiating the Past*, Windhoek, Namibia, University of Namibia Press, 2015. 39ff.

apartheid regime from the 1960s onwards. In this sense it is also apparent that Namibian society is not free of fractures.[83]

83 See Holger Stoecker, 'Knochen im Depot: Namibische Schädel in anthropologischen Sammlungen aus der Kolonialzeit' in: Jürgen Zimmerer (ed), *Kein Platz an der Sonne: Erinnerungsorte der deutschen Kolonialgeschichte* (BPB 2013) 452; see also Krüger, *Kriegsbewältigung* (n 29) 265.

CHAPTER 3

On Legal Reappraisal

Category Genocide

1 A Crime against Human Rights?

Authority over the legal classification of historic events, lies with the *Convention on the Prevention and Punishment of the Crime of Genocide* (CPPCG) of the United Nations (UN). The draft legislation from 1944 is traceable to the Polish-Jewish lawyer and peace researcher Raphael Lemkin. At that time, a description was being sought of the National Socialist crimes, which could not be encompassed by any known category – 'a crime without a name'.[84] From the *γένος* (race, people) borrowed from ancient Greek and the Latin *caedere* (act of killing), Lemkin created the neologism genocide.[85] A legal term for such crimes under international law was unanimously decreed by the UN General Assembly with the UN Convention on 9 December 1948. Article II contains the binding legal definition:

> In the present Convention, genocide means any of the following acts committed with intent to destroy, in whole or in part, a national, ethnic, racial or religious group, as such;
> a. Killing members of the group;
> b. Causing serious bodily or mental harm to members of the group;
> c. Deliberately inflicting on the group conditions of life calculated to bring about its physical destruction in whole or in part;
> d. Imposing measures intended to prevent births within the group;
> e. Forcibly transferring children of the group to another group.[86]

84 Raphael Lemkin, 'Genocide' (1946) 15 *American Scholar* 227. With this he quotes the British Prime Minister Winston Churchill, who described the crimes of the National Socialists thus in a radio speech in 1941. For a different view of Lemkin and his concept: A. Dirk Moses, 'Raphael Lemkin, Culture, and the Concept of Genocide' in Donald Bloxham and A. Dirk Moses (eds), *The Oxford Handbook of Genocide Studies* (Oxford University Press 2010) 19.

85 See Dominik J. Schaller, 'Genozidforschung: Begriffe und Debatten' in Dominik J. Schaller and others (eds), *Enteignet – Vertrieben – Ermordet: Beiträge zur Genozidforschung* (Chronos-Verlag 2004) 11.

86 *Convention on the Prevention and Punishment of the Crime of Genocide*, CPPCG General Assembly of the United Nations, Resolution 260 A (III) of 09/12/1948, entry into force on

 | DOI:10.1163/9789004688209_004

According to this the test criteria that define a group are its victimhood (I.), its (partial) destruction (II.) and specific intent by the perpetrator to exterminate (III.).[87]

I. The Agreement lists national, ethnic, racial or religious groups as protected groups. Political or otherwise identified groups are not included. It is difficult for experts on international law to precisely define these *a priori* vague groups. As social constructs these concepts are inevitably and inherent subjective. In particular, the perpetrators define the status of the individual victims and attribute otherness to them.[88] One solution is to look at the four nominations as complementary, so that they mark out a protected area like corner stones. In reality, it is recognised that they are stable groups, often fixed at birth and unable or unlikely to be changed by its members.[89]

If the Herero and Nama were to be included, they would for instance have to be a national group. This criterion is not met before a state is founded, if a broad interpretation could not be established with a historical and cultural connection.[90] Ethnic belonging is seen today as cultural – via a common language, values, culture.[91] Racial groups have a common origin, physical similarities and geographical closeness, even if the strongly loaded term should only be used 'in the sense of a social group, defined by its somatic appearance'.[92] With regard to religion there was no unity, but the usual characteristics fit. After all, the groups in the course of societal consolidation during the 19th century were stable (see Chapter 2).

---

12 January 1951. In the German Code of Crimes against International Law (CCAIL), the offense is defined in § 6.

87 See Birthe Kundrus and Henning Strotbek, '„Genozid". Grenzen und Möglichkeiten eines Forschungsbegriffs – ein Literaturbericht' (2006) 51 *Neue Politische Literatur* 402.

88 See Joe Verhoeven, 'Le Crime de Génocide. Originalité et Ambiguïté' (1991) 1 *Revue Belge de Droit International* 21; see also William A. Schabas, 'The Law and Genocide' in Donald Bloxham and A. Dirk Moses (eds), *The Oxford Handbook of Genocide Studies* (Oxford University Press 2010) 133.

89 See William A. Schabas and Holger Fließbach, *Genozid im Völkerrecht* (Hamburger Edition 2003) 152; see also Steffen Eicker, *Der Deutsch-Herero-Krieg und das Völkerrecht* (Peter Lang Verlag 2009) 178.

90 See Stefan Glaser in: Nicodème Ruhashyankiko (ed), UN-Study of the Question of the Prevention and Punishment of the Crime of Genocide, Dokument E/CN.4/Sub.2/416 (4 July 1978) <https://digitallibrary.un.org/record/663583/files/E_CN.4_Sub.2_416-EN.pdf>; see Steven R. Ratner, Jason S. Abrams and James L. Bischoff, *Accountability for Human Rights Atrocities in International Law: Beyond the Nuremberg Legacy* (3rd edn, Oxford University Press 2009) 34.

91 See Schabas and Fließbach, *Genozid im Völkerrecht* (n 89) 167.

92 Pierre L. van den Berghe, 'Race – As Synonym' in Ellis Cashmore (ed), *Dictionary of Race and Ethnic Relations* (4th edn, Routledge 1996) 297.

II. The question remains whether these groups have been (partially) destroyed. The CPPCG lists objective elements of crime (*actus reus*). Criminal acts, which could mean the destruction of the group, are listed in Article II. Contrary to the German translation of genocide this does not just include murder (*lit.* a), but also physical and psychological damage (*lit.* b), and/or the deliberate infliction of living conditions that damage the groups physically (*lit.* c).

Did the German prisoner of war policies include such acts? Many of the Herero escaped the siege, even though exact numbers do not exist. It is therefore not certain that the Waterberg offensive fulfilled these conditions.[93] The criteria were, however, met by the subsequent persecution. Even though resistance was not likely, von Trotha ordered the persecution along the borders of the desert with the result of successive exhaustion and dying of thirst. A large number of people were thus killed, others were shot or hanged by soldiers. This type of action can be evaluated as 'destroying the group' (*lit.* a to c), even in cases where some people saved themselves.[94]

In the sense of Article 2 CPPCG the internment in the camps could also be seen as a criminal act. There the prisoners were forced into hard labour. Their existence was marked by the most horrible conditions, resulting in great physical and psychological damage (*lit.* b). For many inmates, the rough conditions proved fatal and can therefore be classified as destructive living conditions (*lit.* c).

Yet the groups of Herero and Nama were not completely exterminated. As macabre as the question may seem, it must be clarified to what extent the offence presupposes a certain number of fatalities. Unfortunately, the death toll amongst the Herero and Name cannot be satisfactorily established with precision. Assessing the pre-war sizes of both groups depends solely on estimates by colonial administrators and missionaries.[95] Due to inaccuracies of the ethnic classification and to nomadic movement, there is considerable uncertainty about the numbers of Herero before the war, said to be between 35,000 and 100,000, of whom, according to estimates, some 14,000 to 16,000 survived. As far as the Nama are concerned, it is assumed that of 20,000 prior to the war, 9,000 to 13,000 survived. The most cautious estimates admit the

93 See Jörn Axel Kämmerer and Jörn Föh, 'Das Völkerrecht als Instrument der Wiedergutmachung? Eine kritische Betrachtung am Beispiel des Herero-Aufstandes' (2004) 42 *Archiv des Völkerrechts* 301.

94 For instance, to Bechuanaland (today Botswana), see Eicker (n 89) 180.

95 For a missionary society Jakob Irle, *Was soll aus den Herero werden?* (Verlag C. Bertelsmann 1905) 5 and also Jakob Irle, *Die Herero: Ein Beitrag zur Landes-, Volks-und Missionskunde* (Verlag C. Bertelsmann 1906) 1.

assumption that at least a third of the population was killed directly or from consequences of war.[96] A more precise determination is not possible, but the question proves to be superfluous. The legal position stipulates, 'The fundamental question is not how many victims were actually killed or injured, but rather how many victims the perpetrator intended to attack'.[97]

III. In this respect, as already required in the chapeau of Article 2 of the CPPCG as a subjective element of the offence (*mens rea*), the casualty figures indicate a tendency where the question of wilfulness (intent to destroy) arises. The actors had to be clearly aware of the aim of the destruction.[98] This had already been indicated by Trotha's racist fantasies of violence and annihilation.[99] The extermination of the Herero and later of the Nama was explicitly ordered in the proclamation: 'Any Herero found within the German frontier, with or without a gun [...], will be executed'.[100] At that, this intent to destroy existed at least between the proclamation in October and its revocation in December 1904.[101]

The aim also proves that all groups were deemed enemies. To be sure, a command of the day ordered the troops to shoot above the heads of women and children.[102] But they too were displaced and died in the process. Many non-combatants were amongst the war victims.[103] The survivors, more than three quarters of them women and children, were collectively interned, including elders. With their herds and the *kraals* (settlements), their livelihoods were attacked.[104]

Even the camps must have been aware of the intent to destroy. One piece of evidence: When asked whether the prisoners should be brought to the

---

96 See Krüger, *Kriegsbewältigung* (n 29) 64; the „Zahlenakrobatik" (number acrobatics) is sharply criticised by Kuß, *Deutsches Militär* (n 39) 86.

97 Schabas, 'Law and Genocide', (n 88) 136.

98 As to intention, Schabas and Fließbach, *Genozid im Völkerrecht* (n 89) 27; John Quigley, 'Intent without Intent' in: Adam Jones (ed), *Genocide in Theory and Law* (Sage 2008) 86.

99 See for example Lothar von Trotha, 'Direktiven für den Angriff gegen die Hereros' (4 August 1904), in *Preußen Großer Generalstab* (n 51) 152.

100 Lothar von Trotha, Proclamation to the Herero people, 2 October 1904 (n 66), source in appendix, 71.

101 See Eicker (n 89) 180.

102 Lothar von Trotha, Additional order, quoted from Rust (n 61) 25.

103 For non-combatants, see Dominik J. Schaller, 'Kolonialkrieg, Völkermord und Zwangsarbeit in „Deutsch-Südwestafrika"' in Dominik J. Schaller and others (eds), *Enteignet – Vertrieben – Ermordet: Beiträge zur Genozidforschung* (Chronos-Verlag 2004) 168 as well as Zimmerer, 'Kriegsgefangene' (n 70) 288.

104 See Jeremy Sarkin, *Germany's Genocide of the Herero: Kaiser Wilhelm II., his General, his Settlers, his Soldiers* (UCT Press 2010) 113.

mainland from the coast on account of the catastrophic conditions, the commander replied that 'as long as he had any say in it, no Hottentot should leave Shark Island alive'.[105] A death rate of 30 to 50, even up to 67 percent is further proof.[106]

The following can be concluded: that I. Herero and Nama were protected groups, which were II. (partially) destroyed, and III. with the intent of complete extermination. No justification for this approach is evident; at the time of the measures to destroy the group, there was no longer any resistance. It is irrelevant whether the group offered negotiations or even submission.[107]

It remains nevertheless to be seen, whether an element of crime according to Article 2 CPPCG exists. A strong applicable *caveat* is quoted: genocide became a human rights violation under international law with the convention of 1948.[108] The paragraph does not have a separate retroactivity clause. It is only possible to create a legal position, which did not exist in the past with retroactive effect, if a new international or customary law has been established, which is not the case here.[109]

For this reason, one opinion sees Article 2 as factually fulfilled but qualifies it the inability to assign blame to the German Empire.[110] The opposing view looks to the legal principles in existence at the time of the crime and sees the act as not factually fulfilled under international law.[111] It is true that the shock waves caused by the atrocities committed by the Turks against the Armenians between 1915 and 1916 can be seen as a beginning of a prohibition of genocide, but this related only to the European zone. Similar problems exist with war crimes and crimes against humanity. The international law experts comment, 'This result, however obvious, leaves a bitter even cynical aftertaste'.[112] Therefore, an extrajudicial evaluation needs to be examined.

105 Berthold von Deimling, in: *Chronik der Gemeinde Lüderitzbucht*, quoted from Zimmerer, 'Krieg, KZ und Völkermord' (n 1) 59. The Dutch pejorative term is still used in idioms today.

106 According to Eicker (n 89) 183, the death rates here are an objective proof.

107 This is also the evaluation of Lemkin in archive manuscripts, which Schaller quotes in 'Kolonialkrieg' (n 103) 229 note 327.

108 Germany ratified the agreement on 12 August 1954, see *Bundesgesetzblatt* II Nr. 15 729.

109 See Patrick Heinemann, 'Die deutschen Genozide an den Herero und Nama: Grenzen der rechtlichen Aufarbeitung' (2016) 55 *Der Staat* 482; see also Kämmerer and Föh, 'Völkerrecht als Instrument' (n 93) 326.

110 Eicker (n 89) 185.

111 Heinemann (n 109) 481 as well as Kämmerer and Föh, 'Völkerrecht als Instrument' (n 93) 314.

112 Kämmerer and Föh, 'Völkerrecht als Instrument' (n 93) 317.

2 Answers Derived from Genocide Research

The category 'genocide' within the comparatively new, interdisciplinary field of genocide research has concentrated on historical, sociological and political scientific perspectives. Classified as an 'Essentially Contested Concept',[113] the term is used there as a subject of discourse and interpretation.[114] With her view of states, structures and situations that enable genocide, Helen Fein's definition is applied to this case.[115]

1. A continuous attack or series of physical attacks must be demonstrated, not simply an action against a society or culture, e.g. the pressure to assimilate. The research has recognised the frequent correlation of war and genocide.[116] In the present case, summary executions were carried out right from the start of the war. However, these were still uncoordinated, single assaults.[117] A systematic strategy was the basis for the attack at the Waterberg Plateau and the persecution in the desert. This includes starving victims to death or poisoning their water. For this reason, letting people die of thirst amounts obviously to an attack.[118] With regard to the camps, reference is made to extermination through neglect,[119] or even through work.[120]

---

113 Engert, 'Politische Schuld' (n 35) 291. Walter Bryce Gallie developed the criteria, which represent such an inherently disputed terms like complexity and openness. Walter Bryce Gallie, 'Essentially Contested Concepts' (1956) 56 *Proceedings of the Aristotelian Society* 167.

114 On the state of the problem Schaller, 'Genozidforschung' (n 85) 14; Kundrus and Strotbek, 'Genozid' (n 87) 397, 420.

115 Here and following Helen Fein, 'Definition and Discontent: Labelling, Detecting and Explaining Genocide in the Twentieth Century' in Stig Förster and Gerhard Hirschfeld (eds), *Genozid in der modernen Geschichte* (LIT Verlag 1999) 18.

116 The cause is the potential for boundary loss, see Daniel Karch, '„Selbst wenn wir sie dabei auslöschen." Entgrenzte Gewalt in der kolonialen Peripherie' (2010) 10 *Jahrbuch für Europäische Überseegeschichte* 115.

117 See Jürgen Zimmerer, 'Bevölkerungsökonomie, Rassenstaat und Genozid' in Wolfgang Benz (ed), *Vorurteil und Genozid. Ideologische Prämissen des Völkermords* (Böhlau Verlag 2010) 17.

118 On the strategy of hunger and thirst until the victims die: Trutz von Trotha, 'Genozidaler Pazifierungskrieg. Soziologische Anmerkungen zum Konzept des Genozids am Beispiel des Kolonialkriegs in Deutsch-Südwestafrika' (2003) 4 *Zeitschrift für Genozidforschung* 54.

119 See Stoecker (n 83) 447; see also Erichsen (n 73) 80.

120 See Michael Brumlik, 'Das Jahrhundert der Extreme' in: Irmtrud Wojak, Susanne Meinl and Fritz Bauer Institut (eds), *Völkermord und Kriegsverbrechen in der ersten Hälfte des 20. Jahrhunderts* (Campus-Verlag 2004) 27. Continuities up to the Holocaust are a subject of their own.

2. A degree of organisation on the part of the perpetrators is assumed, accountability of the state. Genocide involves a political elite gaining or maintaining control.[121] The quest by a colony of settlers for economic exploitation, embellished with ideological and racist arguments, corresponds to this scheme.[122] The question is, who supported extermination as a war objective? Erosion of the limits of violence at the peripheries is largely attributed to the *men on the spot*.[123] But Chief of staff Schlieffen let it be known that the 'racial conflict, which [had] flared up, could only be ended by the extermination or complete enslavement of one of the parties'.[124]

   Kaiser Wilhelm II. had vested von Trotha with absolute power.[125] The soldiers and officers also obeyed, in spite of occasional criticism.[126] There are claims that Chancellor von Bülow had urged stopping the war.[127] This late protest however could hardly exonerate the government – Berlin was complicit.[128]
3. Victims are stigmatised because they belong to a collective. The persecuted are outside what a government deems as belonging. It is against these "essentialised"[129] groups that genocidal acts are absolutely and

121 See Fein, 'Genozid als Staatsverbrechen' (n 115) 38.

122 Melber classifies use of violence as social Darwinist in 'Grenzen des (post-) kolonialen Staates' (n 30) 133.

123 See Karch (n 116) 110; also on the question how far and why the excessive violence escalated. In a wider context of colonialism and genocide, Leo Kuper, *Genocide. Its Political Use in the Twentieth Century* (Yale University Press 1981) 16, 44.

124 Colonel General Alfred Graf von Schlieffen an Reichskanzler Bernhard von Bülow, 23 November 1904, quoted from Frank Oliver Sobich, *„Schwarze Bestien, Rote Gefahr": Rassismus und Antisozialismus im Deutschen Kaiserreich* (Campus 2006) 59; see also Drechsler, *Kolonialherrschaft in Südwestafrika* (n 40) 193.

125 See Kuß, 'Deutsches Militär',(n 39) 88. Trotha, directed by the general staff, was directly subordinate to the Emperor.

126 Representatively Estorff (n 49) 116; see also Zimmerer, 'Krieg, KZ und Völkermord' (n 1) 52.

127 So the memoirs (written much later) of the Imperial Chancellor Bernhard von Bülow, *Denkwürdigkeiten*, Band 2: Von der Marokkokrise bis zum Abschied (Ullstein-Verlag 1930) 21; see also Rainer Tetzlaff, *Afrika. Eine Einführung in Geschichte, Politik und Gesellschaft* (Springer VS 2018) 101 and Boris Barth, *Genozid: Völkermord im 20. Jahrhundert: Geschichte, Theorien, Kontroversen* (CH Beck 2006) 130.

128 See Krüger, *Kriegsbewältigung* (n 29), 62; for the chronological sequence also Sobich (n 124) 59.

129 See von Trotha, 'Genozidaler Pazifierungskrieg' (n 118) 34; see also Helen Fein, 'Scenarios of Genocide. Models of Genocide and Critical Responses' in Israel W. Charny (ed), *The Book of the International Conference on Holocaust and Genocide. Volume 1: Towards Understanding, Intervention and Prevention of Genocide* (Westview Press 1984) 4.

definitively directed, with no escape through conversion or renunciation. Post-colonial theory regards this as a powerful 'othering' practice.[130] If von Trotha's proclamation was 'the Herero are no longer German subjects',[131] they are excluded from the community of those deemed worthy of protection.[132]

4. The degradation endures, even if the victims are no (longer) a threat or they capitulate. The hopelessness of the attacked is emphasised. Thus, the German war conduct is seen by historians from the von Trotha's command onwards as being interspersed with massacres and terror, but even here only as genocidal from the persecution of the victims in the desert onwards. By then the military resistance had been broken.[133] Here too, genocide is not measured in terms of early detection of the number of victims. The reference to the often ignored number of victims who survived is here recognised.[134]
5. In the end, the murders were approved of, indeed intended (once again: *intent*). A handful of documents partly trivialising colonial policies was its gateway. The argument was that von Trotha's proclamation used the term 'extermination' only rhetorically for psychological effect and anyway withdrew it quickly.[135] Another contribution expressed doubts about the intent to annihilate, which questioned the historiography as Eurocentric and claimed the flight of the Herero to be a collective, self-determined exodus.[136] As such argumentation ran the risk of blaming the victims for their fate, objections were raised overall.[137] The campaign

---

130 With regards to the concept, Edward W. Said, *Orientalism* (Pantheon Books 1978) 1, it is also a question of sense of self and of other.

131 Lothar von Trotha, Proclamation to the Herero people, 2 October 1904 (n 66), source in appendix, 71.

132 See Fein, 'Definition and Discontent' (n 115) 19; see also Engert, 'Politische Schuld' (n 35) 290.

133 See Zimmerer, 'Krieg, KZ und Völkermord' (n 1) 50.

134 With regard to numbers of victims, see Fein, 'Definition and Discontent' (n 115) 18; with regard to survivors Mihran Dabag, 'Genozidforschung: Leitfragen, Kontroversen, Überlieferung' (1999) 1 *Zeitschrift für Genozidforschung* 9.

135 Still more scientifically Gunter Spraul, 'Der „Völkermord" an den Herero: Untersuchungen zu einer neuen Kontinuitätsthese' (1988) 39 *Geschichte in Wissenschaft und Unterricht* 723; apologetically Gert Sudholt, *Die deutsche Eingeborenenpolitik. Von den Anfängen bis 1904* (Olms 1975) 184.

136 See Brigitte Lau, 'Uncertain Certainties. The Herero-German War of 1904', *History and Historiography – 4 Essays in Reprint* (1995) 47. Some of her arguments were taken up by right wing viewpoints.

137 Krüger, *Kriegsbewältigung* (n 29) 12 and Tilman Dedering, 'The German-Herero War of 1904: Revisionism of Genocide or Imaginary Historiography?' (1993) 19 *Journal of Southern*

exceeded even drastic ethnic cleansing.[138] The proclamation contained clear proof of the intention to annihilate. By the time the order was rescinded, which was not for humanitarian reasons but in the interest of military strategy, the genocide had already happened.[139] Furthermore, the perpetrators did not deny their actions, but actually praised their effectiveness in the report of the general staff.[140] Even the numerous publications on the subject of the war in the German Empire did not play down these events.[141]

The result is that, according to the criteria examined, a genocide against the Herero and Nama was declared by consensus in genocide research.[142] This debate included an additional two concepts. The term 'colonial genocide' is of unclear origin; it is countered by the argument that this category would lead to regarding non-European history in too much isolation.[143] The label 'genocidal

African Studies 80 were critical. Hillebrecht replied with a pun on the title: 'Certain Uncertainties' or Venturing Progressively into Colonial Apologetics?' (2014) 1 *Journal of Namibian Studies* 73.

138 This is Barth's argument and he classifies the case simply as a case of suspected genocide. Boris Barth, *Genozid: Völkermord Im 20. Jahrhundert: Geschichte, Theorien, Kontroversen* (CH Beck 2006) 128.

139 The reasons were the war against the Nama and lack of troops, see Zimmerer, 'Krieg, KZ und Völkermord' (n 1) 53.

140 Preußen Großer Generalstab (n 51) 173; see Kößler and Melber, 'Völkermord und Gedenken' (n 39) 49. Postcards show the two camps and the dead, see Joachim Zeller, '„Ombepera i koza" Die Kälte tötet mich. Zur Geschichte des Konzentrationslagers in Swakopmund (1904–1908)' in: Jürgen Zimmerer and Joachim Zeller (eds), *Völkermord in Deutsch-Südwestafrika: Der Kolonialkrieg (1904–1908) in Namibia und seine Folgen* (3rd edn, BPB 2016) 67.

141 In some genres, there was a veritable flood of texts that constituted a discourse event. Medardus Brehl, '„Diese Schwarzen haben vor Gott und Menschen den Tod verdient". Der Völkermord an den Herero 1904 und seine zeitgenössische Legitimation' in: Irmtrud Wojak, Susanne Meinl and Fritz Bauer Institut (eds), *Völkermord und Kriegsverbrechen in der ersten Hälfte des 20. Jahrhunderts* (Campus-Verlag 2004) 80.

142 First explicitly voiced by Drechsler, *Südwestafrika unter deutsche Kolonialherrschaft* (n 40) 15; with emphasis agreed Zimmerer, 'Krieg, KZ und Völkermord' (n 1) 52 as well as Kuß, Kundrus, Melber, Kößler and recently Häussler, *Genozid an den Herero* (n 44) 7. Retrospectively, also Helmut Bley agreed, according to Christiane Bürger, *Deutsche Kolonialgeschichte(n): Der Genozid in Namibia und die Geschichtsschreibung der DDR und BRD* (Transcript 2017) 196.

143 Regarding the advantages but especially the disadvantages of the category, Jürgen Zimmerer, 'Kolonialer Genozid? Vom Nutzen und Nachteil einer historischen Kategorie für eine Globalgeschichte des Völkermords' in Dominik J. Schaller and others (eds), *Enteignet – Vertrieben – Emordet: Beiträge zur Genozidforschung* (Chronos-Verlag 2004) 122.

pacification war' is more helpful.[144] Violence is thus classified in the context of domination as an annihilating tool which used massacres and concentration camps as means.

How is the fact dealt with that the term 'genocide' was coined much later? Just as with the genocide of European Jews under the National Socialists, the definition is seen as useful 'in the sense of a historical category for analysis'.[145] This result is particularly important in a political sense.

3 Judicial Reappraisal of the Colonial Injustice

Questions about the evaluation of the events of the war were specifically raised by the fact that from 1999, a Herero representation by Chief Kuiama Riruako, and since 2014 by Chief Vekuii Rukoro, has filed several lawsuits.[146] Initially, the interest group "Herero People's Reparations Corporation" (HPRC), which was founded specifically for legal action, turned to the International Court of Justice (ICJ) in The Hague with a lawsuit against the Federal Republic of Germany as the legal successor to the German Reich. However, as neither individual people nor organisations, but only countries are admitted as claimants, the case was dismissed.[147] The question of who has the right to claim under international law poses a major problem. Individuals do not traditionally have the right to file international legal claims. Although Namibia as a sovereign state has an international identity, it was re-established so that, according to the *Clean Slate Rule,* international law relations began anew; a legal successor does not exist.[148] Even if a court were to go as far as granting the Herero people, partially, the status of legal subject under international law, it would still not be clear whether all Herero or only the descendants of the victims would

144 Trotha, 'Genozidaler Pazifizierungskrieg' (n 118) 30.

145 Zimmerer, 'Krieg, KZ und Völkermord' (n 1) 5.

146 Regarding the reparation claims, Sidney L. Harring, 'The Herero Demand for Reparations from Germany: The Hundred Year Old Legacy of a Colonial War in the Politics of Modern Namibia' in: Max du Plessis and Stephen Peté (eds), *Repairing the Past? International Perspectives on Reparations for Gross Human Rights Abuses* (Intersentia 2007) 437 and Sarkin, *Colonial Genocide* (n 75) 55.

147 See Janntje Böhlke-Itzen, *Kolonialschuld und Entschädigung. Der deutsche Völkermord an den Herero 1904–1907* (Brandes & Apsel 2004) 31; Eicker (n 89) 83.

148 See Lynn Berat, 'Genocide: The Namibian Case against Germany' (1993) 5 *Pace International Law Review* 480 and Heinemann (n 109) 480.

have legal standing.[149] In any case, other groups within Namibia also claimed to have been concerned parties of colonial injustice.[150]

In 2001 the HPRC filed the lawsuit at a district court in Columbia, USA. According to the *Alien Tort Statute* (ATS), US courts can be responsible when foreign citizens claim for prohibited actions outside the USA, as long as international law is deemed broken.[151] As compensation for genocide, crimes against humanity, expropriations and forced labour, claims with regards to payments to victims of Shoah of approximately two billion US dollars were asserted against the Federal Republic of Germany. Additionally, the Herero filed a civil action against German companies at a court in New Jersey in 2006. Another civil class action lawsuit against a bank and company was filed in New York in 2017.[152]

Two of the cases have already been dismissed for lack of jurisdiction. The court referred to its duty of care, saying that offences could only be recognised if there was a sufficient connection to the place of jurisdiction.[153] A possible statute of limitation also caused difficulties. It is true that the claim concerned crimes that are not usually subject to such limitations. However, it was unclear whether this could be transferred to international tort law.[154]

Incidentally, the Federal Republic of Germany had refused to accept the statements of claim, citing sovereign immunity. If a state is sued before the

149 On absent individual claims, Manfred O. Hinz, 'One Hundred Years Later: Germany on Trial in the USA – The Herero Reparations Claim for Genocide', in Eva Schöck-Quinteros and others (eds), *Bürgerliche Gesellschaft. Idee und Wirklichkeit. Festschrift für Manfred Hahn* (Trafo-Verlag 2004) 381; Norman Paech, Der juristische Weg der Wiedergutmachung: Schadensersatz Für Völkermord?' Commentary in Janntje Böhlke-Itzen, *Kolonialschuld und Entschädigung. Der deutsche Völkermord an den Herero 1904–1907* (Brandes & Apsel 2004) 20.

150 See Allan D. Cooper, 'Reparations for the Herero Genocide. Defining the Limits of International Litigation' (2007) 106 (422) *African Affairs* 118.

151 On the law of 1789, see Daniel Felz, *Das Alien Tort Statute: Rechtsprechung, dogmatische Entwicklung und deutsche Interessen* (Duncker & Humblot 2017) 29 as well as Anja Seibert-Fohr, 'United States Alien Tort Statute' in Rüdiger Wolfrum (ed), *Max Planck Encyclopedia of International Law* (2015) para 5. In the 1990s this was a basis for (successful) claims by (descendants of) Holocaust victims.

152 Deutsche Bank was charged with financing the war, the Woermann Line with transport of troops from German ports to South West Africa, the Terex enterprise with profiting from forced labour in railroad construction and mining, Sarkin, 'Colonial Genocide' (n 75) 149.

153 See Felz, *Das Alien Tort Statute* (n 151) 468; see also Hinz, 'One Hundred Years Later' (n 149) 382.

154 See Paech (n 149) 16 and Heinemann (n 109) 474.

court of another state, this recourse is possible. The question of legal dispute is whether this is also the case with the accusation of genocide.[155]

Other grounds for liability are conceivable. The Geneva Convention of 1864, to which the German Empire acceded in 1906, protects wounded soldiers without distinction of nationality, but is an *inter-partes* obligation between the signatory states.[156] Even the Final Act of the Berlin Conference of 1885, which laid down duties of protection and care, does not allow for the Herero to derive their own subjective rights. Neither can The Hague conventions be applied, since there was no armed conflict between independent states. Finally, no breach of the protection agreements with the Herero and Nama can be proved. The mutual assistance treaty, originally external, had been moved into the internal colonial order.[157]

It remains to be determined whether customary international law was breached. One possible legal interpretation, which stipulated the rules of humanity and civilisation, referred without exception to the members of the European community of states. Indigenous (people) were excluded, which explains the lack of international criticism of war and excessive violence in other colonies.[158]

Some authors do not generally consider the legal process to be closed. Their approach is to accept the sovereignty of the Herero and Nama. Thus, an international armed conflict subject to international law is assumed. Reference is made to the Hague conventions of 1899 and 1907 as well as the Martens Clause: Even in cases not regulated by international law, citizens and combatants would be protected by standards of custom, conscience and humanity.[159]

155 Regarding the controversies, see Paech, 'Der juristische Weg' (n 149) 17 and especially Robel (n 21) 312.

156 Geneva Convention (22 August 1864). The objective was to improve the lot of the wounded troops in the field, reference is made here to Article. 6; see regarding the convention, Norbert B. Wagner (ed), *Archiv des Humanitären Völkerrechts in bewaffneten Konflikten*, Band 2/1 <http://www.humanitaeres-voelkerrecht.de/HVR.II.1.pdf> 176.

157 See Kämmerer and Föh, 'Völkerrecht als Instrument' (n 93) 317.

158 See German Bundestag – Research and Documentation Services, 'Der Aufstand der Volksgruppen der Herero und Nama in Deutsch-Südwestafrika (1904–1908). Völkerrechtliche Implikationen und haftungsrechtliche Konsequenzen' <https://www.bundestag.de/resource/blob/478060/28786b58a9c7ae7c6ef358b19ee9f1f0/wd-2-112-16-pdf-data.pdf> 13 as well as Kämmerer and Föh, 'Völkerrecht als Instrument' (n 93) 294. The actions of British forces in Australia and South Africa were not criticised either.

159 A legal process possible, even if very problematic is seen by Sarkin, *Colonial Genocide* (n 75) 88; Rachel J. Anderson, 'Redressing Colonial Genocide. The Hereros' Cause of Action Against Germany' (2005) 93 *California Law Review* 1188 and Malte Jaguttis, 'Koloniales Unrecht im Völkerrecht der Gegenwart' in: Henning Melber (ed), *Genozid und Gedenken.*

However, these remain theoretical contemplations. The appeals court which revisited a claim by the Herero in 2017 decided that the decisions made over 100 years ago by a regime that which no longer exists could no longer be justifiable. As late as March 2019 the most recent claim was rejected. Even when the claimants appealed, the law seemed not to be able to offer clarification.[160]

Thus, beyond the core legal question of the difficult classification in the scope of the later adopted UN Convention, further hurdles remain to legally establishing responsibility.[161] This raises questions about a possible judicial reappraisal. Conventional legal-dogmatic argumentation offers no promise. Will international law reach the limits of its capacity in the case of the Herero and Nama?

The question is which goals are to be achieved with the international (criminal) law classification. The classical function of the law, punishment of those responsible, is excluded. Rather, the descendants of the victims have an expectation of justice for the injustice suffered by their forebears. Yet it is paradoxical that a legal system should grant justice to those whom it excluded from the canon of rules reserved for the European powers.[162]

Court-ordered damages cannot restore the *status quo ante*, nor can they economically measure pecuniary losses suffered in such a way that they could be exactly compensated.[163] These legal functions cannot be fulfilled either. Today's sense of justice would probably prefer to grant the surviving dependants actionable claims on the grounds of decency and balance. This would, however, shatter elementary legal principles (no punishment without law) as well as the possibility of judiciary development.[164]

All in all, the conclusion seems to be that international law as an instrument for compensation is of limited use.[165] Legally, it may be possible to defend

---

Namibisch-Deutsche Geschichte und Gegenwart (Brandes & Apsel 2005) 138 – i.e. non-German authors.

160 See Felicia Jaspert, 'Setback for the Descants of the Nama and Ovaherero Indigenous Peoples' (Völkerrechtsblog, 8 May 2019), <https://voelkerrechtsblog.org/setback-for-the-descendants-of-the-nama-and-ovaherero-indigenous-peoples/> 1.

161 See Jörn Axel Kämmerer, 'Colonialism', in Rüdiger Wolfrum (ed), *Max Planck Encyclopedia of International Law* (January 2018) para. 26; see German Bundestag – Research and Documentation Services (n 158) 15.

162 See Kämmerer and Föh, 'Völkerrecht als Instrument' (n 93) 325; see also Manfred O. Hinz, 'Der Krieg gegen die Herero: Friedensschluss Hundert Jahre danach?' in Norman Paech and others (eds), *Völkerrecht statt Machtpolitik. Beiträge für Gerhard Stuby* (VSA-Verlag 2004) 163.

163 See Harring (n 146) 450; Kämmerer and Föh, 'Völkerrecht als Instrument' (n 93) 326.

164 See Heinemann (n 109) 483.

165 See Kämmerer and Föh, 'Völkerrecht als Instrument' (n 93) 327.

claims for compensation under international law. However, this does not answer the broader question of governmental and ethical behaviour. Ethical and moral demands on contemporary governmental action do not arise exclusively when the act is undoubtedly to be qualified by the UN convention as genocide, indeed: 'the legal finding leaves the great historical guilt of Germany in its moral dimension entirely untouched'.[166] This raises the question of strategies for politically addressing the colonial past in Germany.

166 Heinemann (n 109) 483.

CHAPTER 4

Approaches of Political Reappraisal

1 Forgetting, Suppressing, Avoiding

The end of the German colonial period in 1914 did not mean that this space for projection and fantasy was not used during the time of the Weimar Republic and National Socialism. During the post-war years the colonial past was pushed into the background.[167] In the GDR a narrative of colonial behaviour was used to support political ideological freedom movements in Namibia.[168] Federal West Germany remained mainly silent about the subject in its domestic policies. Before the fall of the Berlin wall, the Holocaust as a breach of 20th century civilisation and after 1990, Stasi and SED injustices dominated the discourse of remembrance. From Namibia itself, occupied and administered by the South African apartheid regime, came no impetus.[169] Neither was Germany encouraged by decolonising eruptions in its former occupied countries to come to terms with the past. Critical post-colonial approaches would be expressed by sporadic local toppling of monuments during the 1970s and 80s, but had no official dimension.[170]

Only the beginning of Namibia's drive for independence brought the subject politically back to the surface in 1989, as part of seeking a position vis-à-vis the newly created state. A debate in the West German Federal Parliament produced in 1989 'a type of constitutional document of German Namibia policy'[171]

167 See Dirk van Laak, 'Deutschland in Afrika. Der deutsche Kolonialismus und seine Nachwirkungen' (2005) 4 *Aus Politik und Zeitgeschichte* 10.

168 See Christiane Bürger, 'Der koloniale Völkermord und die Geschichtspolitik der DDR' (2016) 1 Basler Afrika Bibliographien 3; Helmut Bley and Hans-Georg Schleicher, 'Deutsch-deutsch-namibische Beziehungen von 1960 bis 1990' in Larissa Förster, Dag Henrichsen and Michael Bollig (eds), Namibia – Deutschland, eine geteilte Geschichte: Widerstand, Gewalt, Erinnerung (Ed Minerva 2004) 284.

169 See 'Germany – Namibia. The Belated Apology' (n 15) 132. The renaming (until then *South West Africa*) was the result of a UN decision in 1968.

170 See Robel (n 21) 264. An example: In 1978 unknown persons dissembled the bronze eagle of the 'South West Africa' monument in Göttingen, see Joachim Zeller, 'Andauernde Auseinandersetzungen um das Kolonialkriegerdenkmal in: Göttingen – Eine Chronik' (Freiburg-postkolonial.de, 1 November 2018) <http://www.freiburg-postkolonial.de/Seiten/Goettingen-kolonialadler.htm>.

171 Ulrich Roos and Timo Seidl, 'Im „Südwesten" Nichts Neues? Eine Analyse der deutschen Namibiapolitik als Beitrag zur Rekonstruktion der außenpolitischen Identität des deutschen Nationalstaates' (2015) 4 *Zeitschrift für Friedens-und Konfliktforschung* 193.

DOI:10.1163/9789004688209_005

for cooperation with a new freely-elected government. Whilst emphatic reference was made to the German speaking minority, colonial violence as cause for compensation was not mentioned.[172] Though Germany's special responsibility for Namibia was established, there was no palpable historical reference.[173]

Even after German reunification the Conservative/Liberal coalition went no further in their Namibia policy than maintaining the interests of the German citizens of Namibia. The first and so far only visit by a German head of state, Helmut Kohl (CDU/Conservative), on 14 and 15 September 1995, conveyed the political attitude indirectly, the Chancellor held a reception for several hundred white Namibians and referred to their special services during the development of the country.[174] The march of 300 Herero under Chief Riruako to the German embassy was unexpected. The German Chancellor's delegation was to receive a petition for reparation of 600 million US dollars. Kohl refused any talk. Rejecting any acceptance of responsibility was a political denial strategy.[175]

German President Roman Herzog (CDU), on the occasion of a state visit in Namibia from 4 to 8 March 1998, at least agreed to an – unofficial – meeting, but he rejected any reparation claims with the comment that there could be no penalty without law. This tactic avoided accepting guilt and justified rebuffing any claims.[176] The visit was clouded by the reproach that Herzog had interfered in the country's internal matters.[177]

Even the transition to a Social Democratic/Green federal government in 1998 did not bring about a change. Member of Parliament, Hans-Christian Ströbele (Alliance 90/The Greens) said in 2001, 'that Germany had been lucky early on

172 See German Parliament, document, 15 March 1989, 11/4205, 1; see also Robel (n 21) 274.

173 The burden seemed 'to have grown out of a historical Nirvana'. Janntje Böhlke-Itzen, 'Die bundesdeutsche Diskussion und die Reparationsfrage. Ein „ganz normaler Kolonialkrieg"?' in Henning Melber (ed), *Genozid und Gedenken. Namibisch-Deutsche Geschichte und Gegenwart* (Brandes & Apsel 2005) 114.

174 Kohl addressed the guests with 'Dear fellow countrymen', according to eyewitness Henning Melber: '„Wir haben überhaupt nicht über Reparationen gesprochen". Die namibisch-deutschen Beziehungen: Verdrängung oder Versöhnung?' in: Jürgen Zimmerer and Joachim Zeller (eds), *Völkermord in Deutsch-Südwestafrika. Der Kolonialkrieg (1904–1908) und seine Folgen* (3rd edn, BPB 2016) 220.

175 See Engert, 'Germany – Namibia. The Belated Apology' (n 15) 134, who describes it here as *denial*. Three reactions to political guilt – denial, excuse and apology – are contrasted by Daase, Engert and Renner, 'Guilt, Apology and Reconciliation' (n 4) 4.

176 By the stated rationale, the behaviour would most likely be an *excuse*, see also Stefan Engert, 'Das kollektive Gewissen. Warum Staaten sich (nicht) entschuldigen' in Stephan Schaede and Thorsten Moos (eds), *Das Gewissen* (Mohr Siebeck 2015) 530.

177 Herzog sided with further privileging of the German speakers, which was rejected by President Sam Nujoma, see Kößler and Melber, *Völkermord – Und was dann* (n 22) 49.

to have been forcibly driven out of colonialism' and could therefore take on a role 'with a clean slate and be a trailblazer'.[178] Ursula Eid, the Chancellor's G8 Africa Commissioner said in 2003 that in the view of the suffering of other ethnic groups in the colonial time, it 'would be wrong if the German government "singled out" the Herero for compensation'.[179]

This avoidance behaviour could be seen in other guises too: The president of the German Parliament, Wolfgang Thierse (SPD, social democratic party in Germany), on a visit in Namibia in 2003, did not mention the historical extermination campaign. German Chancellor Gerhard Schröder (SPD), visiting South Africa in 2004, did not feel it worthwhile to make a detour to mark the 100th anniversary of the start of the war.[180]

In 2001, on the occasion of the world conference against racism in Durban, South Africa, Chief Riruako called on the German government, to accept the responsibility, just as it had done in the case of Israel, for the Herero as well; that is to say reparation payments. Then Foreign Secretary, Joschka Fischer (Alliance 90/The Greens) replied to this with general, very vague sounding appeals of personal regret and historical obligation.[181] His Namibian counterpart criticised these comments strongly and accused Fischer of racism for differentiating between black and white victims of German violence.[182]

The real problem to be circumvented, Fischer said in 2003 on his only brief visit to Namibia during his term in office, was possible reparations:

> We are in every way conscious of our historical responsibility, but we are not hostages to history. Therefore, there will be no compensation-relevant apology.[183]

This evasion was in response to the fact that the Herero had also been trying to assert their claim legally since 2001.[184] Behind the topos of relevant

178 Kößler and Melber, 'Völkermord und Gedenken' (n 39) 37. He later changed course significantly.

179 Marc Springer, 'Eid lehnt Entschädigung ab' *Allgemeine Zeitung* (Windhoek, 2 May 2003).

180 See Stefan Fischer and Marc Springer, 'Thierse lobt Namibia' *Allgemeine Zeitung* (Windhoek, 25 April 2003); regarding this journey, see also Kößler and Melber, *Völkermord – Und was dann* (n 22) 52.

181 See 'Fischer bekennt sich zu deutscher Schuld an Sklaverei' *Süddeutsche Zeitung* (Munich, 3 September 2001) 8; see Engert, 'Das kollektive Gewissen' (n 176) 531 and Engert, 'Germany – Namibia. The Belated Apology' (n 15) 133.

182 See Engert, 'Germany – Namibia. The Belated Apology' (n 15) 133 and Kößler and Melber, *Völkermord – Und was dann* (n 22) 51.

183 'Wir sind jetzt am Maximum' *Allgemeine Zeitung* (Windhoek, 30 October 2003).

184 Regarding this 'excuse' strategy – Engert, 'Germany – Namibia. The Belated Apology' (n 15) 134.

compensation was the concern that recognition of colonial guilt could lead to immediate legal enforcement. To avoid payments and also to avoid setting a precedent that could hold other governments or even companies accountable in the future, any admission of guilt was avoided.[185]

2 Development Aid as Compensation?

This policy approach was long used to emphasise the role of Germany as a sponsor of development aid in Namibia, not least in the face of demands for compensation.[186] In fact, since 1990 the country has received approximately one billion Euros and thus receives the most German development aid per capita of any country in Africa (as the population of a little more than two million is comparatively low, this is not a top position in absolute figures).[187] Is development aid 'an indirect form of compensation for (silencing) the past'?[188]

A critical glance at these figures poses the problem that such funds are linked to conditions. With that, the former colonial power still exerts influence. It also furthers the perception that the African continent is in need of aid and development. If a country there is sponsored with voluntary donations, it remains a charitable act by the sponsoring society which maintains its power of control and does not allow the victims the right of distribution.[189] The fact that the conditions in themselves may be sensible makes no difference.

Here Germany also faces an inner Namibian problem. Politically, the state and the largest party, the South West Africa People's Organisation (SWAPO), which has ruled with a dominant majority since independence, are effectively the same.[190] The resources have so far tended to go to their ethnic voter base, the Ovambo. The ethnic groups for which Germany may feel responsible do not receive payments of the same size.[191] A type of deal between the governments

185 See Robel (n 21) 318; Roos and Seidl (n 171) 199.

186 For example, the argument runs through this debate: German Bundestag, plenary protocol, 17 June 2004, 15/114, 10424B. The pattern which was reproduced in the media is analyzed by Robel (n 21) 320.

187 Organization for Economic Co-Operation and Development, 'Creditor Reporting System' (2018) <https://stats.oecd.org/Index.aspx?DataSetCode=CRS1>.

188 Engert, 'Germany – Namibia. The Belated Apology' (n 15) 133. Robel too looks critically at international aid, Robel (n 21) 321.

189 See Jürgen Zimmerer, 'Entschädigung für Herero und Nama' (2005) 6 *Blätter für deutsche und internationale Politik* 658; Böhlke-Itzen, *Kolonialschuld und Entschädigung* (n 147) 101.

190 On the SWAPO party Kößler, *Negotiating the Past* (n 82) 22, 169.

191 See Daase, Engert and Renner, 'Guilt, Apology and Reconciliation' (n 4) 18 on the complex domestic position.

has long been assumed: Through cooperation the Namibian Leadership/SWAPO has been able to strengthen their domestic position, while Germany has been able to rebuff requests for separate compensation with its engagement.[192] In a move not to endanger the great amounts of German aid and also to avoid giving the Herero the monopoly on victimhood, the Herero's demands have long been rejected by the Namibian government.[193] Do the development funds foster discontent?

Another dilemma is the controversial issue of land reform. Since 1990 the government has attempted to offset social inequality by offering to sell land – so far in vain. The Herero and Nama need more money to buy farmland.[194] Suggestions that the intention is to avoid expropriation by force, as in Zimbabwe, carry a certain element of threat.[195] The German government also guarded the interests of Namibians of German origin, who would be harmed by such radical measures, and provided two million euros for land acquisition between 2003 and 2008.[196] However, it must also be remembered that the already privileged whites benefited from this.[197]

Even as development *cooperation*,[198] few bilateral institutions were created which could have effected a different level of cooperation.[199] Consequently, development funds combined with political unwillingness have not achieved any real reparation: In the same period the Herero sued for compensation. Clearly, questions of reappraisal cannot be resolved purely materially.[200]

192 A 'truce': Roos and Seidl (n 171) 204; Kößler and Melber, 'Völkermord und Gedenken' (n 39) 61.

193 See Leonard Jamfa, 'Germany Faces Colonial History in Namibia: A Very Ambiguous "I Am Sorry"' in Mark Gibney (ed), *The Age of Apology: Facing Up to the Past* (University of Pennsylvania Press 2008) 213 and Engert, 'Politische Schuld' (n 35) 297.

194 See Rhoda E. Howard-Hassmann, *Reparations to Africa* (University of Pennsylvania Press 2011) 102.

195 On linking reparation with the issue of land: Kößler and Melber, 'Völkermord und Gedenken', (n 39) 60.

196 See Roos and Seidl (n 171) 204.

197 See Jamfa, 'Germany Faces Colonial History' (n 193) 213.

198 Robel exposes this as a euphemism, wrongly suggesting a partnership, (n 21) 322.

199 Perhaps cultural establishments or agreements, see Jamfa, 'Germany Faces Colonial History' (n 193) 212.

200 See Roos and Seidl (n 171) 195.

3 The 'G-Word' and Breaking Taboos

To forestall any claims, the term genocide was long avoided for political reasons. As recently as June 2004, euphemisms (such as 'the agreed acceptance is that whole groups of the population were exterminated')[201] were preferred – seen as the 'tabooing of the G-word'.[202]

In 2004, the 100th anniversary of the start of the war brought about certain changes. In June, the German Parliament engaged with the remembrance of the victims of the colonial war: This was indeed a milestone. The resolution passed mentioned at least a 'war of extermination'.[203] A change of course became apparent for the green party, who stated, 'We wish to accept and recognise in the German Parliament our political and moral responsibility for all that was committed in the name of Germany for this war of extermination',[204] but did not deem the crimes otherwise.

Against this background, the German Minister for International Development, Heidemarie Wieczorek-Zeul (SPD), elicited surprise with her meaningful words at the remembrance ceremony in Okakarara on the Waterberg Plateau on 12 August 2004: 'The atrocities committed then were what we today call genocide – a General von Trotha would today be brought in front of a court of justice, tried and convicted'.[205] Possibly, the linguistic formulation in the *irrealis* mood was intended to avoid legal implication.[206] Nevertheless, it was so far the clearest official statement. 'I believe that facts remain facts and liability remains liability'[207] she said, declaring her personal motivation to use the historical moment for this acknowledgement.

The taboo of the term "genocide" seemed to have been broken. Yet it is not clear, whether the speech had been agreed with Federal President's office, the

201 German Bundestag, plenary protokol, 17 June 2004, 15/114, 10424A, Ulrich Heinrich (FDP).

202 See Kößler and Melber, *Völkermord – Und was dann* (n 22) 58.

203 German Bundestag, document, 16 June 2004, 15/3329, 1.

204 German Bundestag, plenary protocol, 17 June 2004, 15/114, 10427, Hans-Christian Ströbele (Alliance 90/The Greens). His change of course is very positively described by Kößler and Melber, *Völkermord – Und was dann* (n 22) 41 note 3.

205 Heidemarie Wieczorek-Zeul, Federal Minister for Economic Cooperation and Development, 'Zum 100. Jahrestag der Herero-Aufstände' (Speech at the commemorations, Okakarara, Namibia, 14 August 2004) <https://www.dhm.de/archiv/ausstellungen/namibia/rede.pdf>.

206 See Kößler and Melber, *Völkermord – Und was dann* (n 22) 63.

207 Heidemarie Wieczorek-Zeul, 'In the Words of the Lord's Prayer. Bitte um Vergebung für die Verbrechen an den Nama und Herero', in: Heidemarie Wieczorek-Zeul, *Welt bewegen: Erfahrungen und Begegnungen* (Vorwärts-Buch 2007) 49.

Chancellor's office and/or the Foreign Office.[208] The Foreign Minister was later quoted as saying, 'This is the private opinion of Ms Wieczorek-Zeul',[209] her statement discredited as an individual lapse.[210] On her return, she feared losing her position. In fact, she was able to remain in her post and reinforced her intention for change with a special initiative amounting to 20 million euros for those areas of Namibia which had been particularly harmed by colonialism.[211]

Although the official German policies did not change for several more years, the 2004 anniversary attracted more attention due to the lawsuits filed by the Herero and initiatives from both societies.[212] The Green and Left Parties – whose entry into Parliament brought the debate new momentum – triggered disputes in 2007 and 2008.[213] While these parties advocated for the recognition of the crimes as genocide and for compensation for the Herero and Nama, the other parties argued that the development aid should be seen as reparations already made. Discussion about the use of armed force in the Darfur/Sudan region followed. The risk of a new genocide seemed also to require confronting the past. In contrast, the Liberals' emphasis on the 'challenges of now and today'[214] as a standard sounded like a demand for closure.[215]

Even though the applications were refused, they nevertheless changed the language. Whereas terms like "war of extermination" and "genocide" had until then been avoided in official printed documents, now they appeared in the

---

208 Engert, 'Germany – Namibia. The Belated Apology' (n 15) 136; The German ambassador in Namibia, however, had ruled out an apology, and the Foreign Office had avoided legal documents, Wieczorek-Zeul, 'In the Words of the Lord's Prayer' (n 207) 48.

209 German Bundestag, plenary protocoll, 22 March 2012, 17/168, 19994, Michael Kauch (FDP); see also Kößler, *Negotiating the Past* (n 82) 257.

210 'The emotional outburst of the Minister for Development can cost the taxpayer billions' was the judgement of the CDU/CSU, quoted from Andreas Eckert, 'Der Kolonialismus im europäischen Gedächtnis' (2008) *Aus Politik und Zeitgeschichte* 37; see also Kößler and Melber, *Völkermord – Und was dann* (n 22) 54.

211 See Wieczorek-Zeul, 'In the Words of the Lord's Prayer' (n 207) 49 and Kößler and Melber, *Völkermord – Und was dann* (n 22) 55. The special initiative was raised in 2012 to 36 million euros, according to information from the German Foreign Office, 'Namibia: Beziehungen zu Deutschland' (16 October 2019) <https://www.auswaertiges-amt.de/de/aussenpolitik/laender/namibia-node/bilateral/208320>.

212 See Robel (n 21) 268 – there were initiatives in both countries.

213 The Left Party demanded reparation, German Bundestag, document, 9 March 2007, 16/4649, 1; the Greens called for a parliamentary dialogue with Namibia, see German Bundestag, document, 23 June 2008, 16/9708, 1; see Robel (n 21) 270.

214 German Bundestag, plenary protocol, 13 June 2007, 16/102, 10521, Marina Schuster (FDP): see here as well for the debate of the issue in the Parliament.

215 Kößler and Melber, *Völkermord – Und was dann* (n 22) 64.

filings. Opposition leader Frank-Walter Steinmeier (SPD), too, supported these definitions in 2012 with his party.[216]

In 2014 Horst Köhler, who had retired in 2010 as Federal President of Germany, spoke in the context of European consciousness of the 'genocide of the Herero'.[217] He had already paid special attention to the partnership with Africa during his term in office, but there had been no significant reaction.

The official policy shift was rather understated. At the federal press conference on 10 July 2015 the question was put as to how the Herero-Nama massacre should then be named. The spokesperson for the Foreign Office quoted as an answer the submission, which Steinmeier, then Foreign Secretary, had supported three years previously; according to historical evidence it was now recognised that the war of extermination in Namibia from 1904 until 1908 was a war crime and genocide. This repositioning was so indirect and informal that the journalists had to reassure themselves, 'that sounds like an announcement' – 'well then, announce it'.[218]

This laconic approach points more to a calculated policy adjustment than a fundamental policy shift. Under increasing political-media pressure, continued avoidance ran the risk of the federal government being accused of a flawed moral stance. Rather, a clear designation corresponded to a modern communication strategy of showing openness in "controlled release of air from the attention balloon".[219] Nevertheless, the limits of what the federal government could say politically had clearly shifted.

4 Politicising Colonial Injustice

The decisive driver for the official shift in policy was a different remembrance policy. 2015 saw the 100th anniversary of the massacre and death marches, which in 1915/16 caused the death of up to 1.5 million Armenians, the responsibility for which lay with the Young Turk Revolution of the Ottoman Empire. This, too, was discussed in Germany. Federal Parliamentary President Norbert

216 See German Bundestag, document, 20 March 2012, 17/9033, 1.

217 Horst Köhler, former German President, 'Von der Unmöglichkeit, über Afrika zu sprechen' (Speech on the occasion of the Africa Days of the Ministry of Education and Research, Berlin, 18 March 2014) 3 <https://www.horstkoehler.de/reden-texte/von-der-unmoeglichkeit-ueber-afrika-zu-sprechen/>.

218 Martin Schäfer, speaker of the Foreign Office (n 4).

219 Roos and Seidl (n 171) 213; see also Kößler and Melber, *Völkermord – Und was dann* (n 22) 72.

Lammert (CDU) concluded, 'Whoever speaks in the Federal Republic of the genocide of the Armenians, must not remain silent about the German genocide of the Herero and Nama'.[220] The next day, the language regulation was adjusted to the consensus of the historians. The various memories complemented each other.[221] Publicly, however, there seemed to be no consequences. Faced with the acutely mounting problems in Africa and the streams of asylum seekers in the summer of 2015, the CDU now demanded 'Realpolitik'[222] vis-à-vis the African continent.

On 18 March 2016 the EU countries agreed a convention on refugees with Turkey: the one country in which denial of the Armenian genocide is official policy.[223] In turn, on 2 June 2016 the German Parliament agreed almost unanimously to recognise the massacre of the Armenians as genocide.[224] As the German Empire had been complicit, the members of Parliament had a historic duty to encourage Turks and Armenians to reconcile.[225] However only Gregor Gysi (Left Party) and Cem Özdemir (Alliance 90/The Greens) referred to Namibia and urged the Parliament, 'This genocide too is awaiting reappraisal'.[226]

Because of this historical-political reference, the handling of the colonial injustice evolved into a political issue. Two days after the Armenian resolution, the President of Turkey, Recep Tayyip Erdoğan, denied Germany any right of judgement over Turkey an account of its crimes during the Holocaust and in Namibia.[227] Historically this set the ball rolling.[228] Only days later, Lammert intervened again and demanded the same clarity afforded to genocide of the Armenians for that in the colony. 'I regret, that there is no similar unambiguous

---

220 Norbert Lammert, 'Deutsche ohne Gnade' *Die Zeit* (Hamburg, 9 July 2015) 16; see also 'Bundestagspräsident Lammert nennt Massaker an Herero Völkermord' *Die Zeit* (Hamburg, 8 July 2015).

221 See Robel (n 21) 23.

222 German Bundestag, plenary protocol, 24 September 2015, 18/124, 12091, Bernd Fabricius (CSU).

223 See Joachim Riecker, 'Ja, Völkermord' *Die Zeit* (Hamburg, 1 June 2016).

224 Documented by German Bundestag, document, 31 May 2016, 18/8613, 1. The German chancellor abstained.

225 The German Empire, military main ally of the Ottoman Empire, did not interfere.

226 German Bundestag, plenary protocol, 2 June 2016, 18/173, 17033, Cem Özdemir (Alliance 90/The Greens).

227 'Look at your own genocide history', President Erdogan tells Germany, reported in Daily Sabah (Istanbul, 5 June 2016) an English-language daily newspaper with close ties to Erdogan.

228 See Jürgen Zimmerer, 'Erdogan hat einen Nerv getroffen' *Frankfurter Rundschau* (Frankfurt, 24 June 2016).

explanation on the German side, and in the context of the recent debates it is also a little embarrassing'.[229] The incident made the lack of official declaration in the case of the Herero/Nama clearly visible.

At the very least, the genocide was officially recognised by the government.[230] It was based on the preamble of the UN genocide convention that established that genocide has *at all times* meant great losses. From this the German government concluded, 'For this reason, the definition according to the genocide convention embedded in a historical-political public debate can serve as a benchmark for a non-legal appraisal of a historical event as genocide'.[231]

On an auspicious day, 21 March 2019, the political discourse with the colonial inheritance was debated afresh. It was the Namibian national holiday, precisely one year before the 30th anniversary of the state's founding, when the Left Party began talks about an act of apology.[232] The right-wing Alternative for Germany party (AfD, populist party in Germany) opposed this with an appeal to Namibia to suffer injustice for the sake of peace in the world, as Germany had when it accepted its new borders after 1945.[233] Die Grünen decried all statements justifying colonialism in such terms as attempts at self-justification.[234]

5 German-Namibian Talks

An exegesis of various motions by the SPD, the Greens and the Left revealed that since the commemorative year 2004, reappraisal had been successively considered. Not only official apologies and material compensation were suggested. The parliamentary groups also campaigned to bring colonial history into school textbooks, repatriate mortal remains and establish a bilateral

229 'Lammert fordert Bekenntnis zu „deutschem Völkermord an Herero"' *Der Tagesspiegel* (Berlin, 13 June 2016).

230 See Jürgen Zimmerer and Jürgen Zeller, 'Vorwort' in Jürgen Zimmerer and Jürgen Zeller (eds), Völkermord in Deutsch-Südwestafrika: Der Kolonialkrieg (1904–1908) in *Namibia und seine Folgen* (3rd edn, BPB 2016) 10.

231 German Bundestag, document, 11 July 2016, 18/9152, 3; see Steven Geyer, 'Herero-Massaker. Entschuldigung, aber keine Entschädigung' *Frankfurter Rundschau* (Frankfurt, 3 July 2016).

232 See German Bundestag, plenary protocol, 21 March 2019, 19/89, 10668, Helin Evrim Sommer (Left party).

233 See German Bundestag, plenary protocol, 21 March 2019, 19/89, 10666, Dietmar Friedhoff (AfD).

234 See German Bundestag, document, 21 March 2019, 19/89, 10668, Ottmar von Holtz (The Greens).

parliamentary group.[235] In reconciliation processes, "victims always demanded truth, justice, compensation and the guarantee of non-repetition",[236] so the responsibilities were now framed within *Transitional Justice.*[237]

Across all parties, the efforts for a bilateral dialogue were welcomed. In addition to changed language regulation, the German government started political talks with Namibia in 2015. These were preceded by talks between the two Foreign Ministers in New York. Steinmeier returned in 2013 from the German Parliament to the Foreign Office and nominated as a Special Envoy Ruprecht Polenz (CDU), who had for many years chaired the Foreign Committee in Parliament.[238] He is known for building bridges, for instance with the campaign for Turkey to join the European Union.[239] Since 4 November 2015 he has officially led talks with Namibia to reappraise the colonial past.[240]

Moving between Berlin and Windhoek, once even to Swakopmund, the delegates have so far met eight times. The Namibian delegation, twenty in all, led by the Herero diplomat Zed Ngavirue, includes representatives of the Herero and Nama. One important question of the political engagement is whether Germany has any influence on who will sit at the negotiation table. Polenz distances himself clearly from this: In particular the former colonial power cannot interfere with internal matters of a sovereign state.[241] President Hage Geingob is of the opinion that he represents all Namibians.[242]

Nonetheless, Polenz expresses concern about how a possible negotiated result will be accepted by the Herero and Nama, who are markedly different groups and not always in agreement with each other. The German delegation,

---

235 See among other sources German Bundestag, document, 1 July 2015, 18/5385, 1 and German Bundestag, document, 1 July 2015, 18/5407, 1

236 German Bundestag, plenary protocol, 24 September 2015, 18/124, 12088, Tom Koenigs (Alliance 90/The Greens).

237 See Kößler and Melber, *Völkermord – Und was dann* (n 22) 73 as well as Engert and Jeschke: 'Transitional Justice 2.0' (n 24) 15.

238 See German Bundestag, document, 11 July 2016, 18/9152, 4.

239 Tobias Schulze, 'Reisemuffel und Brückenbauer' *taz, die Tageszeitung* (Berlin, 5 November 2015).

240 Where Ruprecht Polenz is quoted in the following, the statements are taken from the authorised interview with Ruprecht Polenz, official representative of the Federal Government in the dialogue on the genocide of the Herero and Nama with Namibia (Münster, 16 May 2019) transcript in the appendix, 72–79. Direct quotes are always given with page number.

241 Note the sharp clear tone in the interview with Ruprecht Polenz, transcript in the appendix, 74, this was also discussed in the German Parliament, plenary protocol, 21 March 2019, 19/89, 10667.

242 His motto, according to Polenz, was 'We are Namibians!' Interview with Ruprecht Polenz, transcript in the appendix, 74.

with the knowledge of the Namibian side, is trying to address this by holding additional talks with all sectors of society. The Special Envoy also acts as an ambassador both to ethnic groups in Namibia and to elected officials in Germany to promote acceptance of the negotiation process. Polenz explains that success also depends on whether non-political actors like the Namibian Church is willing to signal the spirit of reconciliation to society. Observers see the dilemma about the choice of dialogue partners as the greatest problem.[243]

In terms of content, the drafting of a document aimed at finding a common language about the colonial period was the starting point. This is not just about a basis for parliamentary resolutions. In Polenz's words, 'When we start talking about consequences, we also want to define together from what the consequences will be drawn'.[244] If the crimes are named as genocide in the historical account, this is just as much a milestone as the countries' common view of their history in general, which the talks have already achieved. Difficult moments were described, in particular at the beginning of the talks, when problematic historical comparisons were dealt with.[245]

Beyond that, a renewed commitment to development was negotiated. In contrast to previous payments, the genocide is to be highlighted precisely as the reason for it, and funding is to primarily benefit Herero and Nama descendants, even if such benefits should also be available to other Namibians.

It is emphasised, however, that it is not about reparations in a legal sense, not least with regard to other debates: German talks with Russia about the German siege of Leningrad (since 1991 again named St. Petersburg), or even Greek appeals regarding a forced loan to Nazi Germany. Polenz is *not* aiming for a legal recognition of liability, but a political, moral acknowledgement: 'Therefore, we do not speak of reparations, since that is a legal term, but about what we want to do, what we can do to heal those wounds that may still be open'.[246] Negotiations are also ongoing for a political apology, which may be the most important result of the talk.

---

243 See Kößler and Melber, *Völkermord – Und was dann* (n 22) 85.

244 Interview with Ruprecht Polenz, transcript in the appendix, 72.

245 The issue was the non-comparability with the Holocaust, which Polenz, emphasised, and which the Namibian side perceived as a diminution of their own suffering. See Kößler and Melber, *Völkermord – Und was dann* (n 22) 84.

246 Interview with Ruprecht Polenz, transcript in appendix, 73. The issue of avoiding a "chain reaction" is also described by Angela Köckritz, 'Wie viel darf Versöhnung kosten?' *Die Zeit* (Hamburg, 12 December 2018) 6.

CHAPTER 5

An Ethical and Moral Approach

The Way of Apology

1 Requirements of a Political Apology

In the current negotiations, policy is not limited to development aid, but recognises a far-reaching historical-political responsibility with concrete consequences. The German/Namibian dialogue stands for a fundamental change of perspective. This makes reappraisal not just a defensive '*legal* question, but primarily one of *political* ethical or practical solidarity'.[247] Designation as genocide entailed full recognition of historical liability – less in a legal sense than in its moral meaning – with practical consequences.

In approaching liability in international relations, conflict transformation – the course of *Transitional Justice* – can take various forms. In this case, truth commissions and tribunals are no longer possible for reasons of time, and reparations have been legally excluded.[248] Another means is a plea for pardon as a complex diplomatic speech act. To assess how far this could succeed in the case of the Herero and Nama, the terminology must first be considered.

An apology is a dyadic speech act between a sender and a receiver, whereby the perpetrator admits and regrets damaging and culpable behaviour, acknowledges its often-irreparable harm to the other and regrets this, and makes a promise for the future.[249] If a state acknowledges illegitimately installed authority over a group of victims, this act is translated from the interpersonal to the political sphere.[250] Liability is then publicly admitted in a ceremonial

247 Engert, 'Politische Schuld' (n 35) 294 (highlights in the original).

248 See Christopher Daase, 'Addressing Painful Memories. Apologies as a New Practice in International Relations' in Aleida Assmann and Sebastian Conrad (eds), *Memory in a Global Age. Discourses, Practices and Trajectories* (Palgrave Macmillan 2010) 24; Engert and Daase, 'Aufarbeitung von Schuld' (n 24) 347, 363; for the definition of guilt also: Engert, 'Politische Schuld' (n 35) 294 with reference to Karl Jaspers and Hannah Arendt.

249 Definition according to Engert, 'Staatenwelt nach Canossa' (n 10) 159 and Raymond Cohen, 'Apology and Reconciliation in International Relations' in: Yaacov Bar-Siman-Tov (ed), *From Conflict Resolution to Reconciliation* (Oxford University Press 2004) 177.

250 See Darío Páez, 'Official or Political Apologies and Improvement of Intergroup Relations: A Neo-Durkheimian Approach to Official Apologies as Rituals' 25 *Revista de Psicología Social* 108; Richard Bilder also notes the parallels, 'The Role of Apology in International Law and Diplomacy' (2006) 46 *Virginia Journal of International Law* 464.

symbolic act.[251] An inherent risk is that failure to acknowledge, as well as incomplete or half-hearted acknowledgement, may cause renewed affront.[252]

A successful act of spoken apology must have the following constitutive elements. First and foremost is the complete, detailed description of the offences in terms of extent of damage and violation of the norm. Secondly, a recognition of injustice by declaring responsibility for it. Thirdly, it is of central importance to credibly express regret. The perpetrator must make clear that they would do anything to undo the crimes. Fourthly, compensation to offset the damage the crime caused, and the profit made on account of it. This is less financial compensation as a sign of readiness to bear the material and political costs, thus demonstrating empathy towards the victims. Finally, there must be a guarantee of non-repetition.[253]

The speech act is characterised by its temporal scope with a reference from past to future. The symbolic act of kneeling evokes repentance, penance, contrition and forgiveness.[254] This almost religious component is of great importance. It acts on a psychological level, since the perpetrator asks to be unburdened, the power relation is reversed and in the end, the victim is granted the right to decide over reconciliation. There is a linguistic aspect in the choice of wording and in the fact that the act of speech is only semantically complete when the answer is acknowledged.[255] These dimensions give an apology great potential as an instrument of conflict resolution.[256]

Historical and political context cannot be undervalued. Since the 1990s there has been a change in tendency, so that apologies are being demanded

---

251 See Janna Thompson, 'Apology, Justice and Respect: A Critical Defence of Political Apology' (Australian Association for Professional and Applied Ethics 12th Annual Conference, Aidelaide, 28 to 30 September 2005) 42; Karina Strübbe, *Politische Entschuldigungen: Theorie und Empirie des sprachlichen Handelns* (Springer VS 2018) 118.

252 See Engert, 'Staatenwelt nach Canossa' (n 10) 156; Mihaela Mihai, 'When the State Says "Sorry": State Apologies as Exemplary Political Judgments' (2013) 21 *The Journal of Political Philosophy* 216.

253 These components are listed by Engert, 'Das kollektive Gewissen' (n 176) 518 and Engert, 'Staatenwelt nach Canossa' (n 10) 158; similarly Michael R. Marrus, 'Official Apologies and the Quest for Historical Justice' (2007) 6 *Journal of Human Rights* 79 and Nava Löwenheim, 'A Haunted Past: Requesting Forgiveness for Wrongdoing in International Relations' (2009) 35 *Review of International Studies* 538.

254 For the religious-Christian reference, see Engert, 'Staatenwelt nach Canossa' (n 10) 160.

255 See Engert, 'Das kollektive Gewissen' (n 176) 520; see also Girma Negash, *Apologia Politica: States and their Apologies by Proxy* (Lexington Books 2006) 3.

256 It is a matter of the vulnerability of the perpetrator with regards to the risk of non-acceptance, Engert, 'Das kollektive Gewissen' (n 176) 520; see also Andrieu (n 25) 521.

and offered – even for crimes from very long ago.[257] One reason proffered is political and moral progress, to the point that states must admit their transgressions. These statements, however, are also criticised as superficial rituals of penance carried out for reasons of self-interest.[258] For Germany, the historically great moments show that difficult processes of social reappraisal have accompanied the speech act, while at the same time bringing about unexpected rapprochement.[259]

2 2004 Memorial Ceremony on the Waterberg – 'Forgive Us Our Trespasses'

In the Namibian-German case, of all the approaches to political intercourse, the speech by Federal Minister Wieczorek-Zeul in 2004 was the first to point towards an apology. Beyond naming the crimes as genocide, her act fulfilled other criteria: The blame was laid on the German forces. Regret was expressed in her own name, showing her personal involvement as well as that of German society. Being engaged emotionally elicited empathy and made her words credible.[260] Central to the speech was the petition to the audience:

> I wish to remind us on this day to recall the acts of violence of the German colonial powers, which they committed upon your forebears [...]. I am painfully aware of these atrocities. [...] One hundred years ago

257 Some authors even see an introduction of a completely new age, see Roy L. Brooks, *When Sorry Isn't Enough. The Controversy Over Apologies and Reparations for Human Injustice* (New York University Press 1999) 3; Janna Thompson, *Taking Responsibility for the Past: Reparation and Historical Injustice* (Polity Press 2002) VIII. Amongst many examples are the apology by the Vatican for its passivity during the Holocaust and the apologies by Canada to its *First Nations*, see Cunningham, 'Saying Sorry: The Politics of Apology' (2002) 70 *The Political Quarterly* 285 and Melissa Nobles, *The Politics of Official Apologies* (Cambridge University Press 2008) 155.

258 See Janna Thompson, 'Is a Political Apology a Sorry Affair' (2012) 21 (2) *Social & Legal Studies* 216; Robert R. Weyeneth, 'The Power of Apology and the Process of Historical Reconciliation' (2001) 23 *The Public Historian* 25.

259 These are the (partial) apology for the Holocaust by German Chancellor Konrad Adenauer 1951, the kneeling of German Chancellor Willy Brandt 1970 in Warsaw and the plea for forgiveness to Israel by German President Johannes Rau in Knesset, Israel in 2000. See Engert, 'Staatenwelt nach Canossa' (n 10) 175, 181; Christopher Daase, 'Entschuldigung und Versöhnung in der internationalen Politik' (2013) 25–26 *Aus Politik und Zeitgeschichte* 48.

260 'The emotional agitation in view of the historic moment was obvious; tears came to my eyes'. Wieczorek-Zeul, 'In the Words of the Lord's Prayer' (n 207) 49; see also Kößler, *Negotiating the Past* (n 82) 253, 260.

> the oppressors – blinded by colonial madness – became emissaries of violence, discrimination, racism and destruction. [...] We Germans admit our historical, political, moral and ethical responsibility and the blame, which Germans have brought upon themselves. In the spirit of our shared Lord', I would like to ask you to forgive us our trespasses.[261]

That she, the speaker, does not apologise personally but asks for the debt to be forgiven, is generally seen as essential.[262] Later the speaker explained that she deliberately wanted to build a religious connection with the Namibians, since more than 90 percent are Christian.[263] In fact, requesting forgiveness with an appeal to atonement is said to have the greatest depth.[264]

The speech signalled willingness to take political risks for this apology: At that time, the lawsuit filed by the Herero was already in the courts; the statement could have been taken as an admission of liability. Ultimately there was also a promise of non-recurrence – 'Germany has learned the bitter lessons of history'[265] – and the speaker committed herself to supporting development aid projects.[266]

Nevertheless, the speech was seen by some as a half-hearted, ambiguous apology.[267] The emphasis was on von Trotha as the perpetrator, possibly with the good intention of giving a face to the atrocities. However, this ran the risk of holding an individual responsible for the crimes. It was also highlighted that there had been early opposition to the war: the co-founder of Wieczorek-Zeul's party, August Bebel. Again, it may have been well-meant to underline counter forces, but the argument diminished the extent of the state's responsibility for the calamity.[268]

How the terms "liability" and "responsibility" were used is also problematic: The actual message of an apology was obscured. After her speech had been read out in Otjiherero, voices from the audience asked in English where the apology was. Wieczorek-Zeul added spontaneously, 'Everything I have said

261 Wieczorek-Zeul, 'Zum 100. Jahrestag der Herero-Aufstände' (n 205) 2.

262 See Kößler, *Negotiating the Past* (n 82) 250.

263 See Wieczorek-Zeul, 'In the Words of the Lord's Prayer' (n 207) 49.

264 See Löwenheim (n 253) 537.

265 Wieczorek-Zeul, 'Zum 100. Jahrestag der Herero-Aufstände' (n 205) 2.

266 Engert in particular emphasised the positive aspects of the speech, 'Das kollektive Gewissen' (n 176) 531.

267 See Jamfa, 'Germany Faces Colonial History' (n 193) 212 and Kößler, *Negotiating the Past* (n 82) 247.

268 See Kößler, *Negotiating the Past* (n 82) 258.

in my speech is an apology for the crimes committed by German soldiers'.[269] The fact she could not use the word *in* her speech showed she was walking a rhetorical tightrope.[270]

Moreover, the religious reference – for all its meaningfulness – undermined the speech act because the German government was less implicated.[271] This was made all the more clear by the fact that there was no initial plan for financial compensation.[272] Her good intentions gave the impression of further satisfying the legal and diplomatic imperatives not to open the floodgates for reparations.[273]

The basic problem was that Wieczorek-Zeul did wish to speak in the 'name of the Federal Republic, in the name of the German people and from the heart'.[274] However, her personal courage did not correspond to a coherent political strategy. Neither an act of Parliament nor a statement from the Foreign Office followed. It remained unclear whether it represented a ministerial or official state message.[275]

In Namibia the speech was initially welcomed. However, it led to expectations of compensation, which even a special initiative launched a year later for particularly badly hit areas (not groups) could hardly fulfil.[276] The post-apology actions by a state are of particular importance.[277] Wieczorek-Zeul's requests that the plaintiffs withdraw the legal claims were disregarded. This indicates that the speech was an initiative towards reconciliation at best, but could not be regarded as closure.[278]

269 Wieczorek-Zeul, 'In the Words of the Lord's Prayer' (n 207) 49; see also Kößler, *Negotiating the Past* (n 82) 254.

270 This scene was noted by Kößler, *Negotiating the Past* (n 82) 254; see also Robel (n 21) 334.

271 The speech was a clever way out of state responsibility, according to Tom Bentley, *Empires of Remorse: Narrative, Postcolonialism and Apologies for Colonial Atrocity* (Routledge 2015) 79. Negative aspects of the speech were also addressed, in particular by Jamfa, 'Germany Faces Colonial History' (n 193) 211.

272 Rolf-Henning Hintze, 'Die Deutschen haben eine kollektive Verantwortung. Gespräch mit Johann Galtung' *Allgemeine Zeitung* (Windhoek, 10 March 2006). The peace researcher was visiting the Goethe Institute in Namibia.

273 See Kößler, *Negotiating the Past* (n 82) 260.

274 Wieczorek-Zeul, 'In the Words of the Lord's Prayer' (n 207) 42.

275 See Robel (n 21) 335.

276 See Heidemarie Wieczorek-Zeul, 'Vorwort', in: Reinhart Kößler and Henning Melber (eds), *Völkermord – Und was dann? Die Politik deutsch-namibischer Vergangenheitsbearbeitung* (Brandes & Apsel 2017) 9; Roos and Seidl (n 171) 195 and Robel (n 21) 333.

277 See Mark Gibney und Erik Roxstrom, 'The Status of State Apologies' (2001) 23 *Human Rights Quarterly* 934.

278 See Robel (n 21) 335, quoting a verbal comment by Henning Melber.

3 Non-political Apologies

When the descendants of political war criminals offer apologies, they can establish a very direct connection between past and present. Such efforts exist in the present case. In the commemorative year of 2004, Alfons Maharero met with the family von Trotha, mediated by the evangelical churches of both countries. They are not direct descendants of von Trotha, rather distant relations.[279] For a return visit, eleven members of the von Trotha family travelled to Namibia and were received by five Herero chiefs.[280] Wolf-Thilo von Trotha expressed the family's deep regret and announced their support for a children's home. The family's name was tainted and they were therefore were seeking reconciliation.[281]

But along with the visit came disagreement among the Herero people. Chief Riruako wanted to prevent the visit and threatened he could not guarantee the group's safety, so that they would have to travel with a police escort.[282] On placards, Riruako's group proclaimed that the family could not represent the German government and asked where the families of other colonial actors were.[283] Others recalled the hitherto unfulfilled request for compensation and the desire for talks with Germany. Ulrich von Trotha emphasised that the family was on a private visit in Namibia,[284] which underlined the difficulty of the situation.

Can private initiatives have only limited effect while political questions still remain unresolved? Another non-political apology in particular advocated continuing the path of negotiations started by the governments. In 2017 the German Protestant church presented a document to the descendants of the victims with an admission of guilt and a plea for forgiveness. The role of

279 See Ruben Carranza, Cristián Correa und Elena Naughton, 'Reparative Justice. More than Words: Apologies as a Form of Reparation' (2015) International Center for Transitional Justice Publication, <https://www.ictj.org/sites/default/files/ICTJ-Report-Apologies-2015.pdf> 14. Alfons Maharero is the grandson of Samuel Maharero, revered to this day as a war leader.

280 See Engert, 'Germany – Namibia. The Belated Apology' (n 15) 143 note 37. More details also in Kößler, *Negotiating the Past* (n 82) 193.

281 See Brigitte Weidlich, 'Von Trotha Family Arrives to "Reconcile"' *The Namibian* (Windhoek, 3 October 2007).

282 'Gefährliche Versöhnungsreise' *Süddeutsche Zeitung* (Munich, 7 October 2007).

283 See regarding the visit Reinhart Kößler, 'Offene Wunden – Die von Trotha-Familie beim Herero-Gedenktag 2007 in Omaruru (Namibia)' (freiburg-postkolonial.de, 25 October 2007) <http://www.freiburg-postkolonial.de/Seiten/Rez-2007-Koessler-Hererotag.htm>. Disappointed expectations and excessive demands become obvious.

284 See 'German Family's Namibia Apology' BBC *World News* (London, 7 October 2007).

the missionary organisations, which had provided a theological basis for colonialism, had previously been academically examined.[285] This declaration by the Church indicates that a societal rapprochement has at least begun.

4 Impetus from Political Actors

Another speech can reveal demands for an act of apology precisely in its omissions. More than 70 people from Namibia, some of them direct descendants of the victims, had journeyed to Berlin for a ceremony on 30 September 2011 to return human remains from the collection of the Charité Hospital. During their stay, Namibian officials made it clear that they recognised evidence of genocide in the skulls of the remains.[286] There was no official reception by political representatives of Germany. The whole occasion finally became a political scandal after a speech by Federal Minister Cornelia Pieper (FDP, liberal democratic party in Germany), representing the Federal Government. There was no mention of the circumstances of the deaths of the visitors' forebears.[287] Without even using the word apology, Pieper stated 'On behalf of the Federal government, I wish to ask the Namibian people for reconciliation'.[288] She was met with demands for an apology and left the ceremony before the speeches by the Namibian representatives. The restitution of the remains was considered a failure.[289]

Was it first necessary to break taboos for a speech act to be successful? A new opportunity presented itself around Hamburg, where between 1904 and 1907 almost all soldiers, goods, horses and artillery had been shipped to South West Africa. A large share of the city's wealth stems from colonial networks. Since 2013, Hamburg has engaged in a city-wide initiative of remembrance, including a university research centre. Its congress offered the opportunity to

285 German Protestant Church (Evangelische Kirche in Deutschland, EKD), 'Vergib uns unsere Schuld (Matthäus 6, 12)' EKD-Statement in regard to the genocide in former German South West Africa (24 April 2017) <https://www.ekd.de/ekd_de/ds_doc/erklaerung_voelkermord_deutschsuedwestafrika.pdf>.

286 The circumstances were described by Stoecker (n 83) 453.

287 See Kößler and Melber, *Völkermord – Und was dann* (n 22) 65.

288 Cornelia Pieper, German Minister of State, 'Speech on the occasion of the Ceremony for the handover of skulls of Namibian origin in the Charité (Speech in the Charité' in Berlin, 30 September 2011) <https://www.auswaertiges-amt.de/de/newsroom/110930-stmpieper-rede-hereronama/247300>.

289 See Kößler and Melber, *Völkermord – Und was dann* (n 22) 65; see also interview with Ruprecht Polenz, transcript in appendix, 75.

officially receive a Herero and Nama delegation in the Senate on 6 April.[290] Culture Senator Carsten Brosda (SPD) stated,

> I expressly ask your forgiveness for the involvement of our city in the harm that your forebears and peoples suffered in the name of Germany and the devastating consequences of which still reverberate today.[291]

This approach was adopted sometime later by another state politician, this time from Berlin. As the capital of the German Empire, from where the decisions of the general staff about the war had been taken, Berlin was the political power centre of colonialism. On 27 August 2018, in the context of another repatriation of remains, the Senator for Justice for Berlin, Dirk Behrendt (Alliance 90/ The Greens) welcomed members of the victims' associations. He too spoke for his city, 'On this day, I am able to and wish to apologise on behalf of Berlin'.[292]

The contents of these acts of speech fulfilled important criteria. However, they were delivered by state politicians who could speak for their cities but not for the Federal Republic. The higher the rank of the speaker in the political hierarchy, the more credible the apology. This is important both to adequately represent society and to assure that the political system supports the apology.[293] It can be assumed that these apologies were intended to bear a message to political Berlin, where Behrendt worded this appeal carefully, 'It would be in the interest of a democratic and constitutional Federal Republic of Germany to finally accept these crimes as such and take responsibility for them'.[294]

At the actual restitution ceremony, the Federal Minister for Cultural and Educational Policy, Michelle Müntefering (SPD), gave a speech; her department had just put the raising of colonial consciousness[295] on its agenda. A religious setting, the French Friedrichstadt Church, was chosen as the venue.

---

290 Axel Schröder, 'Wir werden kämpfen bis die Gerechtigkeit siegt' *Deutschlandfunk Kultur* (Berlin, 7 April 2018).

291 Quoted from Elisabeth Knoblauch, 'Aus der Heimat entführt, um Europa zu amüsieren' *Die Zeit* (Hamburg, 6 December 2018) 8; see also Jan Haarmeyer, 'Stadt entschuldigt sich bei Herero-und Nama-Opferverbänden' *Hamburger Abendblatt* (Hamburg, 6 April 2018).

292 Katrin Bischoff, 'Justizsenator bittet Opferverbände um Verzeihung' *Berliner Zeitung* (Berlin, 28 August 2019).

293 See Daase, 'Addressing Painful Memories' (n 248) 26; see also Carranza, Correa und Naughton (n 279) 13.

294 See Paul Starzmann, 'Berliner Justizsenator bittet Herero und Nama um Entschuldigung' *Der Tagesspiegel* (Berlin, 27 August 2019).

295 In particular on the cultural-political reappraisal of colonialism, Monika Grütters und Michelle Müntefering, 'Eine Lücke in unserem Gedächtnis. Gastbeitrag' *Frankfurter Allgemeine Zeitung* (FAZ) (Frankfurt, 15 December 2018).

She described the crimes, pointing out the complete lack of respect towards human beings, and referred to them as not only a historical-political but also a moral-ethical responsibility. To limit the damage, more histories of origin had to be researched and restitutions planned. A promise for the future pointed to a German/Namibian dialogue. Finally, in a gesture of humility, the speaker put her repentance into words,

> I bow to you in profound sadness. I cannot undo the terrible wrong our forebears have done to you. But I beg you from the bottom of my heart for your forgiveness.[296]

This speech was seen as a milestone on the road to reappraising German colonial injustice. But it still was not the apology of a highest-rank representative of Germany, for which many people in Namibia are urgently waiting.[297]

5 Prospects of a Plea for Forgiveness

According to chief negotiator Ruprecht Polenz, the clock for reappraising the historic conflict has been ticking now for thirty years. Only with the independence of Namibia and the end of the apartheid system came the opportunity for a direct relationship. Through bilateral dialogue, mutual steps to approach this part of Germany's difficult, violent past are finally possible. Polenz draws a parallel to talks held with Israel, Jewish organisations, Poland, France and the Netherlands in the course of confronting the Holocaust. This reflects the larger context in which the negotiations are taking place.

Thus the German/Namibian talks also have at their core a political apology. Polenz said in an interview,

> Germany wishes to request forgiveness for the crimes committed in those times. Obviously, we cannot forgive ourselves, but instead we ask forgiveness and hope that the other side grants it. For the other side, it

296 Michelle Müntefering, German Minister of State, 'Rückgabe sterblicher Überreste an Namibia' (Speech at the restitution and commemoration ceremony in the Französische Friedrichsstadtkirche, Berlin, 29 August 2018) <https://www.auswaertiges-amt.de/de/newsroom/muentefering-namibia/2131046>.

297 Christiane Habermalz, 'Meilenstein im Prozess der Aufarbeitung deutscher kolonialer Schuld' *Deutschlandfunk* (Cologne, 29 August 2019) and Susanne Klein, 'Bitte um Vergebung' *Süddeutsche Zeitung* (Munich, 29 August 2018) 6.

> is important to know whether this plea for forgiveness is in earnest or just a matter of words, so that they can decide it can be accepted. And that can be answered by asking what will follow this plea for forgiveness. Our negotiations focus on this question: What will follow the plea for forgiveness.[298]

With this Germany stands at a historical turning point to politically confront the legacy of its colonial past, which it is accepting some 100 years later. Whether the presented criteria for a speech act have any prospect of being fulfilled with an apology towards the descendants of the victims in Namibia is thus considered below.

A comprehensive record of the crimes is essential. Therein lies the great value of the elaborated joint declaration on the historical events. The injustice committed, the damage caused are thereby recognised, expressly as a parliamentary document.[299] This would also have to establish the responsibility of the German Empire – not only of the "Protective Forces" or von Trotha.

A newer contribution questions whether Germany is able to admit responsibility for the crimes against the Herero and Nama. It reasons that Germany today is not equivalent to the German Empire. Only the perpetrators themselves have the capacity and authority to fully accept their liability.[300] This argument overlooks the argument that there is a legal continuity between the two states.[301] Furthermore, a state can see itself as a polity, which does not just pass on successes but also responsibilities to subsequent generations.[302]

At the core of the speech act is an expression of regret. Polenz stated on the record: We want to convey to the descendants that we are sorry for the crimes today; we cannot undo them, but we can do as much as possible for a good future relationship. This goes beyond regret to symbolise contrition and is closely connected with the real attempt to at least mitigate the damage today. The fact that it is subject to negotiation is criticised by some because a

298 Interview with Ruprecht Polenz, transcript in the appendix, 72.

299 Legal standards can help to identify injustice, according to Löwenheim (n 253) 540.

300 See Anna Kietzerow, 'When a State Should Not Apologize' (Presentation at the annual conference of the International Society for Military Ethics in Europe (EuroISME), Vienna, 23 May 2019) 15.

301 See Kößler and Melber, *Völkermord – Und was dann* (n 22) 118; see also Engert, 'Politische Schuld, moralische Außenpolitik?' (n 35) 295.

302 See Thompson, 'Apology, Justice and Respect' (n 251) 38.

negotiated apology seems less effective. By contrast, a collaborative resolution allows the parties concerned to speak for themselves.[303]

The negotiators recognised that compensation is a necessary step. The measures to be financed by Germany include help for the professional training of youth, support for affordable housing, improvements to the health system and supplying renewable energy. Furthermore, land reform is to be supported to retain an important source of income for Namibia: in the words of Polenz, safety in the country is essential for tourism, which is why expropriation should be prevented at all costs. Compensation will not be on an individual, but a collective basis with the objective of improving the quality of life for the victims' descendants.

Finally, there must be a guarantee of non-recurrence. The German delegation has introduced the discussion about founding a German/Namibian foundation for the future, to enshrine the shared history in schoolbooks and the curriculum, to bring commemoration into the public sphere and to initiate a youth exchange program. This last has been understood correctly by Namibia as a reference to 'Action Reconciliation Service for Peace', a German peace organisation of international volunteer programs. Besides educational strategies it is concerned with mutual experiences and relationships. With this comes the promise that lessons have been learned from history.[304]

Apart from these excellent prospects of a possible speech act however, there are some concerns. As can be seen in the previous approaches, only the very highest state representative can sufficiently represent the country which committed the crimes.[305] It has not yet been decided whether the Chancellor as head of government or President Frank-Walter Steinmeier as head of state, whose engagement has already been mentioned, should become involved. Both have assured the chief negotiator Polenz of their willingness to do so. Then it will be important to find the proper symbolic language for both cultures as well as time and location.

The act of speech must also enjoy societal acceptance in the country of the sender. The more acceptance, the more certain the receivers can be sure of a

303 Critical, Kößler and Melber, *Völkermord – Und was dann* (n 22) 118; approving, Thompson, 'Apology, Justice and Respect' (n 251) 42.

304 See interview with Ruprecht Polenz, transcript in the appendix, 77. What it means to change the viewpoint in the culture of the perpetrators, Jean-Michel Chaumont, *Die Konkurrenz der Opfer: Genozid, Identität und Anerkennung* (zu Klampen 2001) 311.

305 See Daase, 'Addressing Painful Memories', 26 with regards to status and role as decisive factors.

consistent political stance.[306] Public requests within Germany for an apology imply that society would support the act; however, comments in media fora advise scepticism.[307] It has not yet been decided whether the use of taxpayer money will be approved (Polenz has not been able to reveal a financial framework). The German coalition government will then have the task of communicating the purpose of reappraising colonialism.

The Special Envoy, faced with the demand for a speedy apology, has requested more time: This places less pressure on the German government than on the Namibian negotiator. A ceremony can only take place once the dialogue has been concluded, for this the country needs time. Polenz had hoped in vain to complete this process before the Namibian elections at the end of 2019. Neither did the trip of then Federal Minister for Economic Cooperation and Development, Gerd Müller (CSU), to Namibia on 29 August 2019, nor the celebration of 30 years of Namibia's independence on 31 March 2020 set the wheels in motion.

Finally, one factor is of the greatest importance. Almost at the same time as the interview, experts wrote a letter to the German government expressing concerns about growing tensions within Namibia. They acknowledged that Germany could not directly influence internal Namibian affairs. However, they advise using transparency and participation as decisive means to create further opportunities for dialogue involving the various victim groups and civil society. Cultural, educational and social structures could open up such spaces.[308] If not all of the Herero and Nama were included, the voices against compromise would grow in strength. This would bring real danger of illegal land occupation and vigilante justice, in which Germany would be complicit.[309] This appeal must be considered during the current efforts.

---

306 On encouraging factors Engert, 'Das kollektive Gewissen' (n 176) 518 and Daase, 'Addressing Painful Memories' (n 248) 26.

307 Posts, mostly anonymous, often relativise the crimes by pointing to other colonial powers or set out absurd arguments – for instance, that at the crusades would also require an apology.

308 See Jürgen Zimmerer and others, 'In großer Sorge um den Aussöhnungsprozess mit Herero und Nama: Brief an Bundeskanzlerin Angela Merkel' (Hamburg, 2 April 2019; open letter published 10 May 2019) <https://www.kolonialismus.uni-hamburg.de/wp-content/uploads/Brief-BKA-und-AA.pdf>.

309 See Jürgen Zimmerer, 'Commentary on the publication of the Open Letter' (Hamburg, 10 May 2019) <https://www.kolonialismus.uni-hamburg.de/2019/05/10/offener-brief-an-die-bundesregierung-genozid-an-den-herero-und-nama/>.

Conclusion

1 Summary

Assessing the judicial, political and ethical reappraisal of the genocide has required study of historical sources, a critical review of international law, an assessment of development aid policy, a review of political debate and finally a change of perspective toward an ethical and moral understanding, and to once more highlight important dimensions. In doing so, this paper has taken an interdisciplinary approach to a highly topical subject.

It was necessary to begin the historical overview with the establishment of German rule, to expose the economic, political and social destruction of African societies as reasons for the outbreak of war. The proclamation to the Herero was proof of the boundlessness of violence. The summary of the horrors does not just include the dead, who made up a large part of the population. The camps, too, meant the continuation of mass killing. The consequences of the war (distribution of land, demography) are felt up to the present times.[310]

This has been the basis for investigating whether the legal definition of genocide has been met – a core issue of the debate. The criminal liability of these deeds, committed with the intention to destroy national, ethnic, racial or religious groups wholly or partially, was determined in 1948 by the United Nations. This paper has highlighted the problem that this ban did not exist at the time of the acts. In contrast, it was shown that research establishes genocide (a series of attacks for which the state is responsible, and which seeks to destroy a collective of victims beyond military defeat)[311] to be proven by historical analysis.[312]

The legal channels of action have been considered with this background. If there had already been legal problems in the inter-temporal application of international law, then sovereign immunity, limitation and jurisdiction of the courts proved to be yet further obstacles. As a result, international law proved to be an unsuitable means of dealing with historical injustice in this case. The mere clarification of how an act was legally assessed at the time of the crime cannot define behaviour according to today's values.

310 See Stefan Engert, 'Politische Schuld' (n 35) 291 as well as Kößler and Melber, 'Völkermord und Gedenken' (n 39) 50.

311 See Fein, 'Definition and Discontent' (n 115) 18.

312 See Zimmerer, 'Krieg, KZ und Völkermord' (n 1) 5.

This was followed by the question of how the political community dealt with the historical past. It was pointed out that political representatives long took little notice of the colonial legacy. Foreign Minister Fischer contrasted the legal complaints, which may have exerted political pressure, with the fact that there would be no 'compensation-relevant' apologies.[313] The paper has critically examined development aid, as it also proved inadequate as a gesture of reconciliation. The linguistic breaking down of taboos regarding use the term genocide in the political arena was also pursued. Historical-political interactions could be shown concerning the commemoration of the Armenian genocide. Finally, the study provided insights into the German-Namibian talks on reappraising their shared history.

Thus, the perception of the colonial past is no longer determined in legal terms, but moral standards. Therefore, the question arose, whether an apology by the state for the harm done to the victims and their descendants is an adequate means of transitional justice. To this end, the components and scope of such a speech act have been considered. The requirements for the use case were drawn up from the achievements and deficiencies of previous approaches. As the interview demonstrates, Germany wishes apologise to the descendants of the victims and to materially mitigate the harm done. Therefore, it was examined to what extent the apology speech act has a good chance of being fulfilled. There were doubts in particular regarding the inclusion of all persons concerned.

2 Policy Recommendation

The current negotiation results are currently being reviewed by the respective governments. This paper recommends that German side acknowledge the genocide historically and politically, morally and ethically accept responsibility for it and offer a credible apology to the groups concerned. It is also recommended that structures be established in consultation with the Namibian government to ensure the involvement of all concerned parties in Namibia, but possibly also of civil societies in Namibia and Germany: This churches, who have already been working for reconciliation, can assist in this.

Such an enterprise has great potential to prepare the ground for reconciliation in the difficult diplomatic and domestic Namibian situation. Apologies

313 'Relevant for compensation – an expression as if carved from German oak' caricatured Bartholomäus Grill, 'Aufräumen, aufhängen, niederknallen!' *Die Zeit* (Hamburg, 5 August 2004) 10.

are not limited to the past. Amongst the transitional justice approaches – processes and practices that support the transition from violence to peace – apologies set themselves apart from retributive procedures (criminal prosecution) that wish to close the books. With their relevance to the present and their aspirations to form the future, they operate within the scope of restorative justice, which sets out to realign the relationships of those involved.[314]

Such a step also has internal importance. Germany is changing into a heterogeneous, multi-ethnic society. People arriving from Africa have perhaps experienced the consequences of colonialism from the other side.[315] This gives rise to the political and social task of breaking down old patterns of power and superiority. Polenz says, 'In dealing with people of different colour, we still have much to learn, even now'.[316] The fact that the town of Eisenberg in June 2019 renamed their town fair 'Mohrenfest' (festival of the moor), in spite of the protests of the Initiative of Black People in Germany, is an example of the need to rethink.[317]

Also, apology is no longer seen in the Western world as breaking taboo. Facing up to one's own past is a growing trend. In Burkina Faso in November 2017, French President Emmanuel Macron announced the restitution of the French collections of African art within five years.[318] In the best case, a critical approach to one's own history is not only a core part of Germany's self-image, but also of a self-reflective European consciousness.[319] Internationally, Germany could take a pioneering role and, for manageable cost, set a sign that African concerns are taken seriously, and that reappraisal of the past is a key issue for the future.[320]

Finally, apologies are seen by the international community of nations as a form of reparation. The United Nations has established that in the case of violations of international law, state responsibility includes restoration of

314 See Andrieu (n 25) 5 and Engert, 'Politische Schuld' (n 35) 281. Recognizing that apologies follow their own logic are Martha Minow, Between Vengeance and Forgiveness: Facing History after Genocide and Mass Violence (Beacon Press 2009) 114 and Nicholas Tavuchis, Mea Culpa: A Sociology of Apology and Reconciliation (Stanford University Press 1991) 5.

315 Gernot Knoedler, 'Umbenennung ist richtiger Schritt. Interview mit Jürgen Zimmerer' *taz, die Tageszeitung* (Berlin, 11 September 2013).

316 Interview with Ruprecht Polenz, transcript in appendix, 77.

317 'Eisenberg feiert trotz Kritik „Mohrenfest"', *Mitteldeutscher Rundfunk* (Erfurt, 22 May 2019). (Mohr = derogatory name for a black person).

318 Emmanuel Macron, President of France, 'Discours de Ouagadougou', (Speech at the University of Ouagadougou, Burkina Faso, 28 November 2017) <https://www.elysee.fr/emmanuel-macron/2017/11/28/discours-demmanuel-macron-a-luniversite-de-ouagadougou>.

319 On German reason of state Kößler and Melber, *Völkermord – Und was dann* (n 22) 79.

320 See Howard-Hassmann (n 194) 101.

the *status quo ante*, financial compensation, and non-material satisfaction. 'Satisfaction may consist in an acknowledgement of the breach, an expression of regret, a formal apology or another appropriate modality'.[321] This underlines the significance of the speech act as a diplomatic convention. The state is able to prevent escalation and introduce negotiations.[322] The present case has shown that states may not ask for forgiveness for fear of legal consequences, when in fact formal apologies and the correct follow-up could replace the legal route.[323] A new international standard could solve this dilemma.

3 Other Means of Reappraisal

The plea for forgiveness could provide impetus for a reappraisal of the colonial past on other levels. Perhaps the most obvious 'commemorative corrections' are the renaming of streets.[324] In many places, the colonial Empire was manifested through street names in the motherland, something criticised only since the 1980s in the former West Germany by post-colonial initiatives at a local level, not infrequently with a reference to contemporary racism.[325] There were protests, for example, about Munich's Von-Trotha-Straße. When the city administration renamed the street after the aristocratic family of the same name, the debate did not end. In 2007, the street was renamed Herero-Straße.[326] Renaming seems particularly inappropriate with highly problematic names. Instead, communities could discuss *whom* they actually want to

---

321 Commission for International Law of the United Nations, Draft Articles on Responsibility of States for Internationally Wrongful Acts, UN-Document A/56/10 (2001 / 2008) <https://legal.un.org/ilc/texts/instruments/english/commentaries/9_6_2001.pdf> 105.

322 See Bilder (n 250) 464; see on the speech act in diplomacy Engert, 'Staatenwelt nach Canossa' (n 10) 156.

323 The complexity is described by Arthur Watts, 'The Art of Apology' in Maurizio Ragazzi (ed), International Responsibility Today. Essays (Martin Nijhoff 2005) 107; see also Bilder (n 250) 471.

324 Jürgen Zimmerer, 'Kolonialismus und kollektive Identität: Erinnerungsorte der deutschen Kolonialgeschichte' in Jürgen Zimmerer (ed), *Kein Platz an der Sonne: Erinnerungsorte der deutschen Kolonialgeschichte* (BPB 2013) 21.

325 Examples are Lüderitzstraße, Mohrenstraße or Windhukstraße (in old-German spelling). See Joachim Zeller, 'Zwischen Wilhelmshaven und München: (Post-)Koloniale Erinnerungskultur in Deutschland' in Ulrich van der Heyden and Joachim Zeller (eds), Kolonialismus hierzulande: Eine Spurensuche in Deutschland (Sutton 2007) 271 as well as Speitkamp (n 19) 419.

326 The confronations are described by Ulrike Lindner, 'Das Kolonialviertel in München-Trudering' in Ulrich van der Heyden and Joachim Zeller (eds): Kolonialismus hierzulande: Eine Spurensuche in Deutschland (Sutton 2007) 296.

memorialise.[327] Even if names are kept in order not to erase the past, information boards can constitute post-colonial places of learning.[328]

In such cases, the intention of the government to raise awareness for the colonial heritage through support of local initiatives and authentic memorial sites can be useful.[329] Creating historical awareness is particularly effective when it involves local residents, the Black community and representatives from Namibia.[330] This applies all the more to the need for a central memorial to crimes that were committed so far away.[331]

The repatriation of human remains is already underway. Insufficient documentation, difficulties with conservation and the respective context of injustice present ever greater obstacles for the anthropological collections still in existence today. Provenance researchers must particularly carefully verify individual identities and/or ethnic affiliations – for the purpose of repatriation.[332] For indigenous communities, such stories offer better opportunities to engage than the many anonymous remains.[333] In one case, a Herero skull in possession of a family only arrived in Namibia after more than ten years of efforts.[334] Would a point of contact make sense in such cases? Restitution processes in both countries can be the catalyst for important commemorative discourse.

327 A good example: 'An wen wollen wir (uns) erinnern? Der Streit um Namensgebungen im öffentlichen Raum. Live aus dem FHXB Friedrichhain-Kreuzberg-Museum Berlin' *Deutschlandfunk* (Berlin, 5 December 2018).

328 This began in the African Quarter in Berlin, 1899 with 25 streets referring to South West or Africa. Today, steles explain the backgrounds, see Alexander Honold, 'Afrikanisches Viertel. Straßennamen als kolonialer Gedächtnisraum', in Birthe Kundrus (ed): Phantasiereiche. Zur Kulturgeschichte des deutschen Kolonialismus (Campus 2003) 307.

329 See Coalition agreement (n 12) 157; also about such monuments Speitkamp (n 19) 409.

330 See Kößler, *Negotiating the Past* (n 82) 74; see also Kößler and Melber, *Völkermord – Und was dann* (n 22) 128.

331 See Christiane Habermalz, 'Koloniales Nicht-Gedenken in Deutschland' *Deutschlandfunk* (Cologne, 16 February 2018).

332 Stoecker (n 83), 442 in particular describes collections and transfer routes for Berlin; a journalistic approach is offered by Michael Stang, 'Leichen im Keller – Vom Umgang mit kolonialen Skelettsammlungen' *Deutschlandfunk Kultur* (Berlin, 14 April 2016).

333 See Gesine Krüger, 'Knochen im Transfer – Zur Restitution sterblicher Überreste in historischer Perspektive' in: Holger Stoecker, Thomas Schnalke and Andreas Winkelmann (eds), Sammeln, Erforschen, Zurückgeben? Menschliche Gebeine aus der Kolonialzeit in akademischen und musealen Sammlungen (Links 2013) 488 and Anna-Maria Brandstetter, 'Provenienz (Un)Geklärt – Und Was Dann? Einführung' in Larissa Förster and others (eds), Provenienzforschung zu ethnografischen Sammlungen der Kolonialzeit: Positionen in der aktuellen Debatte. Elektronischer Tagungsband (Arbeitsgruppe Museum der Deutschen Gesellschaft für Sozial-und Kulturanthropologie 2018) 189.

334 Christoph Titz, 'Herr Ziegenfuß ist den Schädel los' *Der Spiegel* (Hamburg, 28 August 2018).

The same applies for the repatriation of colonial cultural goods. In February 2019, Baden-Württemberg returned the Bible which had belonged to Nama Chief Hendrik Witbooi to the Namibian government. It had been kept for more than one hundred years in the Linden Museum in Stuttgart. But the Nama too had declared their claim and applied to the constitutional court of Stuttgart to suspend its repatriation. The difficult question has not yet been answered of how state institutions can return stolen goods without interfering in internal matters or causing disputes between a government and the society of origin. The next restitution is expected in May 2019. The board of trustees of the German Historical Museum in Berlin have agreed to return the Cape Cross Column to Namibia.[335]

Fur such questions (concerning the Humboldt Forum Berlin,[336] a guideline for dealing with the colonial collections of the German Museums Association)[337] debate needs to be deepened. Museums, arts and science offer great hope for transnational rapprochement.[338] Universities can take steps toward scientific reappraisal, even with regard to their own role as institutions. The work of one research centre in Hamburg[339] also takes on political (its initiative led to the Senate reception of the Herero/Nama delegation) and cultural dimensions (it was a partner in a German/Namibian art project).[340]

Finally, the Chamber of Commerce in Hamburg has begun a historical reappraisal by cataloguing its archives and holding a series of events. Alongside politics, science and culture, the economy is addressed as a sub-sector facing the difficult questions regarding its own role in colonial interdependencies and power structures.[341]

---

335 The beacon of Portuguese conquerors was stolen by the German navy. Birgit Rieger, 'Die Säule von Cape Cross geht zurück an Namibia' *Der Tagesspiegel* (Berlin, 18 May 2019) 25.

336 See the series of talks, 'Das Humboldt-Forum und seine Geschichte(n)', *Deutschlandfunk* (Cologne, 2019).

337 German Museum Association (Deutscher Museumsbund), 'Guidelines for the Care of Collection from Colonial Contexts' (English version, 2021) <https://www.museumsbund.de/publikationen/guidelines-on-dealing-with-collections-from-colonial-contexts-2/>.

338 See Rebekka Habermas, Ulrike Lindner, 'Rückgabe – und mehr!' *Die Zeit* (Hamburg, 13 December 2018) 19.

339 Project Association Research Center Hamburg's (post-)colonial legacy/Hamburg and early Globalization' <https://www.geschichte.uni-hamburg.de/arbeitsbereiche/globalgeschichte/forschung/forschungsstelle-hamburgs-postkoloniales-erbe.html>.

340 Exhibition 'Ovizire. Somgu, From Where Do We Speak? Von Woher Sprechen Wir?' Museum am Rothenbaum, Kunst und Kulturen der Welt (MARKK) and art salon M. Bassy in cooperation with the University of Hamburg (Hamburg, 4 December 2018 until 14 April 2019).

341 See Knoblauch (n 291) 8.

4 Outlook

This paper could be followed by the Namibian perspective on the steps of reappraisal. In this context it would have to be clarified how the effectiveness of political apologies could be recorded empirically.

From a political standpoint, Cameroon, under often brutal German rule from 1884 until 1919, could be the next country in focus for compensation.[342] At the same time, it puts the case of this study in a different context. The questions addressed here also transcend the individual case in the course of transformative reappraisal of the past and postcolonial communication.[343]

The colonial "Protective Forces", the subject of the photograph in the preface, is no longer justifiable today, no matter how it may have been historically, legally or politically. It will be watched with keen interest whether and when Germany will put forward a plea for forgiveness to the descendants of the victims in Namibia and what the reaction will be. With that, the perspective of the victims would finally be ethically and morally recognised. This paper has also revealed the difficulties associated with such a historical reappraisal. Nevertheless, the transformative potential of this method of transitional justice carries within it the great hope that far-reaching processes of reconciliation can begin.

---

342 Maria Ketzmerick, 'Postkoloniale Außenpolitik: Wie sich Deutschland in Kamerun engagieren sollte' (PeaceLab-Blog of the Global Public Policy Institute Berlin, 20 May 2019). <https://peacelab.blog/2019/05/postkoloniale-aussenpolitik-wie-sich-deutschland-in-kamerun-engagieren-sollte>.

343 See Kößler and Melber, Völkermord – und was dann (n 22) 117.

Afterword

When this thesis was completed in July 2019, diplomatic talks between Germany and Namibia (alternately in Windhoek and Berlin) on how to address their shared history were still in progress. In the following, developments up to July 2022 are briefly presented and recommendations for possible further developments are outlined.

After nine rounds of talks, the German-Namibian dialogue process has now ended. On 15 May 2021, the draft joint declaration of the Republic of Namibia and the Federal Republic of Germany entitled "United in remembrance of our colonial past, united in our will to reconcile, united in our vision of the future" was presented.[344] Provided the declaration is signed, the German government would thereby firstly acknowledge moral responsibility for the colonisation of Namibia, the grave human rights violations and genocide. Secondly, Germany would accept the moral, historical and political obligation to apologise for this genocide. Thirdly, a support programme of 1.1 billion euros over 30 years would be launched in the regions of the particularly affected population groups.[345]

The agreement has been strongly criticised by several Herero and Nama interest groups. "The German Government acknowledges that the abominable atrocities committed during periods of the colonial war culminated in events that, *from today's perspective, would be called genocide*",[346] reads one contentious passage. This is seen as a tactic to continue to avoid legal obligations. The sum of the payments is also deemed to be too low. In general, many groups do not feel adequately included in the dialogue process, as only some of the many groups concerned sat at the negotiating table. In view of inequalities in post-colonial Namibia, bilateral talks at the state level have been rejected. The minorities do not feel represented by their government and therefore doubt that the financial aid will reach the most affected communities, especially in view of the high level of corruption in Namibia. Instead, direct compensation to the victims' descendants is demanded. Paramount Chief Vekuii

344 'Versöhnungsabkommen mit Namibia – Deutschland erkennt Kolonialverbrechen als Genozid an' *Deutschlandfunk* (Cologne, 21 September 2021).

345 A review of the agreement with Namibian and German voices: Henning Melber and Kristin Platt (eds), *Koloniale Vergangenheit – Postkoloniale Zukunft? Die deutsch-namibischen Beziehungen neu denken* (Brandes & Apsel 2022).

346 Joint Declaration by the Federal Republic of Germany and the Republic of Namibia (June 2021), <https://www.dngev.de/images/stories/Startseite/joint-declaration_2021-05.pdf> (Emphasis added by the author).

© EURO-ISME, 2024 | DOI:10.1163/9789004688209_008

Rukoro – the traditional leader of the Herero and Ovaherero, but with disputed authority within the ethnic groups – announced opposition to a visit by German President Frank-Walter Steinmeier as head of state.[347]

The German chief negotiator, Ruprecht Polenz, said that at the moment one can only wait for the reaction of the Namibian government. However, he was also concerned about a long delay in implementing the agreement. According to Polenz, there will be no renegotiation. By insisting on bilateral talks at the state level, Germany had respected Namibia's sovereignty. In addition to the critical voices, Polenz also recognises those who are clearly in favour of the negotiation process. He sees one possibility for resolving the conflict in bringing forward disbursements. So far, the two governments have not signed the declaration.[348]

In June 2021, Namibia was afflicted by a catastrophic wave of Covid-19 infections. Zed Ngavirue, Herero and Namibian government negotiator with Germany – and key advocate for the negotiation process – died of Covid-19, as did two of the agreement's fiercest critics, Paramount Chief of the Herero Vekuii Rukoro and Gaob Eduard Afrikaner of the Nama Traditional Leaders Association. Other actors also fell seriously ill. Due to the pandemic, important votes on the outcome of the negotiations in the Herero and Nama communities could not be conducted. As a sign of Germany's willingness to accept responsibility in the present, vaccine supplies were introduced into the dialogue.[349]

Vaccines against Covid-19 have indeed been donated by the federal government, although no information as to quantities has been made available. More than a year later, the proportion of people in Namibia who have been fully vaccinated against Covid-19 is just under 20 percent. Previously, the German government had already supplied respirators and other medical items. The pandemic also brought tourism, the most important source of income for the

---

347 The NGO alliance "No Amnesty on Genocide!" has compiled many assessments under the title "Our colonial present': <https://genocide-namibia.net/2021/06/liste-von-meldungen-und-analysen-zum-versoehnungsabkommen/#page-content>. See also Jürgen Zimmerer, 'In kolonialen Spuren. Warum ein Versöhnungsabkommen ohne Zustimmung aller Herero und Nama kein Grund zum Feiern ist', mission-lifeline.de, <https://mission-lifeline.de/juergen-zimmerer/>.

348 See Heiner Hoffmann, 'Streit über Versöhnungsabkommen mit Namibia. „Moral ist nicht weniger wert als Recht". Interview mit Ruprecht Polenz' *Der Spiegel* (Hamburg, 9 October 2021).

349 Christiane Habermalz, 'Deutschlands Rolle in Namibia – Impfen zur Versöhnung?' *Deutschlandfunk* (Cologne, 5 July 2022).

Namibian economy, to a virtual standstill. Financial aid was provided to alleviate the economic and social impacts of the crisis.[350]

Due to the highly charged Covid-19 situation, parliamentary debate on the proposed joint agreement in Namibia was postponed until September 2021. Hundreds of people demonstrated against the agreement in front of the Namibian parliament in Windhoek with placards, whistles and chants. Protesters broke through a barrier and some of the scenes were tumultuous. The controversial parliamentary debate remained inconclusive.[351]

At virtually the same time, German President Frank-Walter Steinmeier affirmed the task of reappraising colonial history in Germany as a task for society as a whole: In order to overcome discrimination, diminution and physical attacks in the present, colonial history must be brought to the forefront of public awareness. "The truth is: when it comes to the colonial era, we Germans, who are otherwise so historically aware, are all too lacking in knowledge! We have blind spots in our memory and our self-perception".[352] Nigerian writer Chimamanda Ngozi Adichie, one of the most important African voices, captured the image: "We cannot change our past, but we can change our blindness to the past."[353]

A new federal government has been in office in Germany since the end of 2021. The coalition agreement states: "Reconciliation with Namibia remains an indispensable task for us, which arises from our historical and moral responsibility. The reconciliation agreement with Namibia can be the prelude to a joint process."[354] A statement by the Federal Foreign Office reads: "A central

350 Foreign Office of Germany, 'Namibia: Beziehungen zu Deutschland' (Berlin, 21 December 2021) https://www.auswaertiges-amt.de/de/aussenpolitik/laender/namibia-node/bilateral/208320.

351 Paul Starzmann, 'Muss das Völkermord-Abkommen mit Namibia neu verhandelt werden? Herero und Nama protestieren gegen Deutschland' *Der Tagesspiegel* (Berlin, 22 September 2021).

352 Frank-Walter Steinmeier, German President, 'Eröffnung der Ausstellungen des Ethnologischen Museums und des Museums für Asiatische Kunst der Staatlichen Museen zu Berlin' (Speech at the ceremony in the Humboldt Forum, Berlin, 22 September 2021) <https://www.humboldtforum.org/de/programm/digitales-angebot/digital/festrede-von-frank-walter-steinmeier-33700/>.

353 Chimamanda Ngozi Adichie, 'Eröffnung der Ausstellungen des Ethnologischen Museums und des Museums für Asiatische Kunst der Staatlichen Museen zu Berlin' (Speech at the ceremony in the Humboldt Forum, Berlin, 22 September 2021) <https://www.humboldtforum.org/de/programm/digitales-angebot/digital/festrede-von-chimamanda-adichie-32872/>.

354 'Daring more progress'. Coalition agreement between the SPD, Alliance 90/The Greens and the FDP for the 20th legislative period of the German Bundestag (Berlin, 7 December

concern in bilateral relations is reappraising the atrocities committed against the Herero and Nama peoples under German colonial rule in the former colony of German South West Africa during the war of 1904 – 1908."[355] Both documents suggest that the reconciliation agreement is understood as only the beginning of further steps towards reparations in the direction of meaningful reconciliation.

The Namibian leadership has announced its readiness to restart negotiations. In the case of a political apology, the decision on the next steps is indeed up to the aggrieved parties, who alone can judge how much time is needed. This would be a way out of the dilemma. Perhaps German Foreign Minister Annalena Baerbock can break the stalemate.[356]

However, this would also require agreement between individual groups within Namibia. The parties are to some extent divided and fragmented. Who will sit at the negotiating table is an essential question. A sobering interim outcome of the dialogue process is therefore that bilateral talks alone cannot achieve their objectives if only one government, which does not have the confidence of all the people, chooses the negotiating partners.

There are various projections on what developments in addressing historical colonial injustice and violence appear possible in the future. The statement by former German Foreign Minister Joschka Fischer that there would not be a "compensation-relevant apology" has already been cited.[357] Presumably no precedent should be set for dealing with other violent events – in the former colonies or during the occupation of Europe in the Second World War – for reparation claims. With this position, the genocide was not labelled as such.

A contemporary witness to the violent crimes against the Herero and Nama, on the other hand, presents a completely different picture. During a Reichstag debate in December 1905, the SPD Member of the Reichstag Georg Ledebour said of the commander General Lothar von Trotha and the governing Reich Chancellor Bernhard von Bülow:

> But the two gentlemen who have so far proved that they did not know how to properly uphold German honour in waging war against barbarian

2021) <https://www.bundesregierung.de/breg-de/service/gesetzesvorhaben/koalitionsvertrag-2021-1990800> 126.

355 Foreign Office of Germany (n 350).

356 Henning Melber and Jephta Nguherimo, 'Reconciliation is Different. The Flaws in the German-Namibian Joint Declaration on the Genocide' *The Namibian* (Windhoek, 17 December 2021).

357 See 'Wir sind jetzt am Maximum' (n 183).

> tribes do, however, belong in the dock, before the judgment seat of the German people and the judgment seat of history, and whatever they may say: the German people and history will find them guilty.[358]

Today, Namibia and Germany are faced with the choice of which of the two predictions will eventually come true. The historical record clearly demonstrates the grave crime of exterminating the ethnic groups and depriving them of their livelihoods. During the lifetimes of the perpetrators, there were no legal proceedings and thus no judgment of guilt. With the final agreement on the German-Namibian dialogue process, a request for forgiveness by the German head of state is a prospect for the first time. This offers hope that the violence and injustice will be condemned politically and socially.

Reappraising the past is based on the recognition that the objective cannot be achieved by taking a single step, but requires comprehensive, complex processes full of disruptions, learning curves and efforts that ultimately never end. A request for forgiveness can be a milestone on a path, in a labyrinth of paths. As Ledebour propounded, Germany – through politics and society – would have to condemn the violence, find the perpetrators guilty and stand with the victims.

In order to appropriately address colonial violence, it must be possible in the future to adequately involve the descendants of the victims in the process without imposing conditions on the former colony. Could an agreement be reached with the Namibian government to directly involve indigenous peoples in the question of funding distribution? Is it possible, with their consent, to involve churches and communities, museums and universities, economic actors and cultural institutions as stakeholders? Its responsibilities lie in various forms of cooperation, in commemorative culture, in repatriating looted colonial property, in creating awareness of colonialism, in dialogue and rapprochement through reconnecting people. The list is not exhaustive.

The task only appears too difficult to accomplish. "Solutions always start with dialogue," said Herero youth activist Ileni Henguva at a recent debate between the young Herero generation and German Namibian landowners.[359] Seeing eye-to-eye points the right course.

---

358 Stenographic report on proceedings in the Reichstag, 2 December 1905, XI. Parliamentary period, V. session, vol. 214, 1906, 92/B, Georg Ledebour. The Social Democrats applauded.

359 Claus Stäcker, 'Genozid-Debatte in Namibia,' *Deutsche Welle* (Berlin / Bonn, 18 March 2022).

Appendix

1 Source – Proclamation of General von Trotha

Proclamation to the people of the Herero
Copy of the original.
17290 Osombo-Windembe, on 2nd October 1904 High Command of the Protection Force.
'I, the great general of the German soldiers, send this letter to the Herero people. The Herero are German subjects no longer. They have killed, stolen, cut off the ears and other parts of the body of wounded soldiers, and now are too cowardly to want to fight any longer. I announce to the people that whoever hands me one of the Chiefs shall receive 1,000 marks, and 5,000 marks for Samuel Maherero. The Herero nation must now leave the country.

If it refuses, I shall compel it to do so with the 'long tube'.[360] Any Herero found inside the German frontier, with or without a gun or cattle, will be executed. I shall spare neither women nor children. I shall give the order to drive them away and fire on them. Such are my words to the Herero people.

The great General of the powerful German Emperor.

This proclamation is to read to the troops at roll-call, with the addition that the unit that catches a Captain will also receive the appropriate reward, and that the shooting at women and children is to be understood as shooting above their heads, so as to force them to run [away]. I assume absolutely that this proclamation will result in taking no more male prisoners, but will not degenerate into atrocities against women and children. The latter will run away if one shoots at them a couple of times. The troops will remain conscious of the good reputation of the German soldier.

The Commander
Signed, von Trotha, Lieutenant General.'

Source
Michael Behnen (ed), *Quellen zur deutschen Außenpolitik im Zeitalter des Imperialismus 1890–1911* (Wissenschaftliche Buchgesellschaft 1977) 291; text also in Conrad Rust, *Krieg und Frieden im Hererolande: Aufzeichnungen aus dem Kriegsjahre 1904* (Kittler 1905) 25.

360 This means 'cannon', author's note.

2 Interview

Name:	Ruprecht Polenz
Organisation.	Christian Democratic Party of Germany (CDU)
Function.	Special Envoy of the German Government for the German/ Namibian negotiations concerning the shared colonial past
Place:	Münster, Germany
Date:	16th May 2019

Can you introduce yourself in the position you now occupy in relation to the negotiation process?

I have been Special Envoy for the German/Namibian negotiations about the shared colonial past since November 2015. After having been on the Foreign Affairs Committee for twenty years until 2013 and chairing the Foreign Affairs Committee for the past eight years, Mr Steinmeier asked me to take on this duty, to which I agreed. The negotiations, which I have led since December, had begun on a working level several months previously and the reason for involving me was to put them onto a political level.

Where are the negotiations right now, what would be a snapshot?

We have met eight times, alternating between Berlin and Windhoek, and once in Swakopmund, and we have worked through a negotiation programme that we agreed at the very beginning; we want to conduct the negotiations, and have managed to do so, as win-win negotiations, because both sides rightly say: the German/Namibian relationship is a good one, but there is one point from the past that we must speak about so that we can develop the relationship further. That has always hovered over us as a question not properly addressed.

Which question was that?

The question of the crimes between 1904 and 1908. The negotiation programme we agreed upon could be summarized this way: We want to describe the events of those times in a shared language, not to rewrite history but to have a shared starting base. This is so that, when we start talking about consequences, we also want to define together from what the consequences will be drawn. The paper should also serve as a basis for parliamentary resolutions, which is why it is kept short. We have almost completed writing. By my guess, it consists of approximately 8 pages, describing what took place then, and to answer one question straight away: the crimes committed against the Herero and Nama are named as genocide.

The second point is: Germany would like to request forgiveness for the crimes committed in those times. Obviously, we cannot apologise and leave it at that, but instead we ask for forgiveness and hope that the other side grants it. For those on the other side, it is important to know whether this plea is in earnest or just a matter of words, so that they can decide whether a plea for forgiveness can be accepted. And that can be answered when looking at the question: What will follow this plea for forgiveness. And our negotiations focus on this question: What will follow the request for forgiveness.

From our point of view, we are dealing with a political and moral question, not a legal issue that can be decided by the courts. That has been learned from the past, since there have been three unsuccessful lawsuits. Naturally, however, the political and moral question remains, which is no less important than the legal question, but it is nevertheless different. Therefore, we are not speaking of reparations, since that is a legal term, but about that what we want to do, what can be done to heal those wounds that may still be open. That is not using legal language, but it describes precisely what is at stake here.

How would you describe the process of the negotiations?

We have been meeting with a delegation of the Namibian government, led by Dr Ngavirue, a Herero. There are between ten and twenty people on the Namibian side, it varies from time to time. There are Herero and Nama present, as well as members of the government. On our side I am supported by the director for Sub-Saharan Africa in the Foreign Office, currently Robert Dölger, his predecessor was Georg Schmidt, the head of division from the Department for International Law, Ms Bauch and our ambassador in Windhoek, Mr Schlaga. We prepare these negotiations by communicating the agenda to each other, then work through it, which takes approximately one and a half days. However, on my visits to Namibia, I generally spent three to four days there and used the remaining time – the Namibian government was informed of this – to speak to as many interested parties in Namibia as possible. I also spoke with those who were involved in the lawsuit in New York: I met Mr Rukoro, I met Ms Hoffmann[361] as well as old Mr Frederiks.[362] I met members of the Witbooi family and various Herero groups, as well as different members of the Namibian-German community, the white Namibians, and formed my own opinions, but on the other hand I used these conversations for what I am currently relating to you, that is to say what the process is all about and what is actually happening, so that no one gets the impression we negotiated behind closed doors, not taking into account everyone's own interests.

I find it very interesting that you are now, if I understand rightly, a form of ambassador of your own negotiating process?

361 Ida Hoffmann, Member of Parliament and chair of the Nama Genocide Technical Committee in Namibia, author's note.

362 David Frederiks, Nama Chief, died in 2018, whose forbears fought in the war, author's note.

I made that very clear, since I have given several interviews. I was particularly pleased by the interest of 'Deutschlandfunk' (a German public radio broadcaster), which gave the report more space, but also by one or the other newspaper, even international newspapers and I have always pointed that out. I don't know how often it was included in the reports, but I believe that is the process.

Who is present at the negotiating table – could you describe the difficulties and decision-making processes, which have to be negotiated?

It is important to note that the decision of who participates was not negotiated by Germany and Namibia, because in such negotiations each side always chooses its own delegates. It is as simple as that. Somehow, Germany finds it difficult to accept that. During a briefing of Parliament commissions, with whom I am in regular contact, one of the Members of Parliament, I believe from the Left party, asked why we did not make sure that others, perhaps in the current case representatives of Herero and Nama, were sitting here amongst the others at the table, so I replied: You know, if I represented the Namibian government and Germany came forward with this request, I would ask quite brusquely if they had not realised that Namibia is no longer a German colony.

Nevertheless, this question comes up again and at its core is a real concern, that is to say, whether the result will be accepted by the Herero and Nama, for we all wish, because we want to set a broad reconciliation process in motion, so to speak, through the outcome of the negotiations afterwards. So it is important how the overall negotiation results are received.

To understand the Namibian position, we must remember that Namibia has been independent since 1990. Since then the SWAPO has governed the country and made great efforts to impart a national consciousness, a sense of patriotism that states: We are not a collection of various tribes living next to each other but 'We are Namibians'. For this reason, the president emphasises that he represents all Namibians, including the Herero and Nama, and therefore does not appreciate the urgency that some actors, who may not completely trust the government, place on tribal representation. And I found during my visits to Namibia that there are at least three different groups of Herero who are not necessarily in accord with each other: the green, the red and the white Herero. The same goes for the Nama.

Everyone who thinks they should be entitled to decide who sits at the table and makes decisions and who does not should look again at the repatriation of the Witbooi Bible. That was a lengthy process. The Witbooi Bible was owned by the federal state of Baden-Württemberg and after long negotiations Baden-Württemberg and the museum that had it agreed to return the Bible. All preparations were made for the Minister of Culture of Baden-Württemberg to hand over the Bible during a ceremony to the President of Namibia. To stop this, Mr Rukoro and probably part of the Witbooi family tried to obtain a provisional order not to return the Bible, at least not to the government, because there were private ownership claims. Luckily the Supreme Court of Baden Württemberg refused to grant this order, and the Bible was returned.

Symbolically it was of great interest: the Bible was physically handed to the President who immediately passed it on to his Minister for Culture and Education, who took it upon herself to find its proper place. How this will be arranged is up to the Namibians themselves. However, if – and that is why I am telling this story – we had tried to decide ourselves who is the most appropriate person to whom to hand this Bible we had in our possession, there would probably have been five or more pairs of hands reaching out for it. And we would not have had an option to decide who is best. In that case, the Bible would most likely have stayed in Germany. This way the Bible is where it belongs, i.e. in Namibia and it is up to the Namibians to decide how to deal with this very important document of their history.

And the issues we are currently negotiating are similar. Take the issue 'healing of the wounds'; I shall tell you that we put great emphasis on the descendants of the Herero and Nama, so that they above all have the benefits. How? On the one hand we support vocational education so that young people will have greater opportunities, we are looking at affordable accommodation, a functioning health system, electricity supply using renewable energy and we also assist with the land reform which is handled by Namibia itself. That is a chapter in its own right.

Does that answer the question about exactly what is being negotiated?

Yes. And there is another very important matter, the repatriation of human remains. There had been two repatriations before my time, whereby the first went badly wrong because a chain of circumstances led finally to a rather undignified procedure. The second one was more successful and the third, which we worked on very carefully last year with the generous help of the German Protestant Church and the Council of Namibian Churches, to create a setting in Berlin and Namibia for the reception of these human remains, went well and all were very satisfied with it. This is not an end to the matter, since there are still human remains in Germany. Finding them is an ongoing task, but in any case, we have found a way to repatriate the remains in a dignified way which is accepted by all parties.

And besides that there is a task to develop a shared culture of remembrance in both countries in the future – we have still not achieved this. For this we suggested founding a German-Namibian Trust for the future, similar to the one we have with the Czech Republic. There could be shared schoolbook projects, agreeing on how these times and the history are presented, as we did with Poland and France with very good results. The crux is remembrance in the public sphere, which is always the case in Namibia whilst in Germany it is somewhat shamefaced and not always appropriately observed.

To this end we have also suggested a youth exchange. When we mentioned this in a conversation, Bishop Kameta, the Minister for poverty eradication said, 'Ah, like Action

Reconciliation Service for Peace – yes, that I can see working'. The Namibians were very keen on this idea and we have made great progress with this matter. The input did not come just from us but from documents that were given to us by the Namibians regarding their negotiation positions, during preliminary stages and during the course of the negotiations – we asked what we could do and then they made suggestions, we made suggestions, that is how it developed. And now I would say the result has so far reached an intermediate appraisal stage with both governments, so that we are in a position to know what still needs negotiating and what has been resolved.

It is difficult to predict how long this process will last. There is in any case a certain impatience, which I feel in Germany too, because they we really like to request forgiveness. Of course, it is possible to do this right away, but then there is the problem that occurred with the previous requests for forgiveness or declarations of apology, that the Namibian side is not content with this type of apology, for it leaves unanswered the question 'And what now?'. But because it has become urgent and everyone is looking for closure, there is a certain amount of impatience. Mr Zimmerer, whom you perhaps know, gives an interview on this subject once a month. However, I do not think it appropriate to put such pressure on the Namibian government. To me it sounds as if as if we are trying to say, 'Hurry up, we want to finally apologise and be done'. And even in a matter such as this one, that is not the way to behave with a partner.

I understood from the press that it was Germany which was under pressure.

We are not under pressure because we were actually in a position to act fast. No one on the Namibian side is claiming that we are playing for time. It is of no interest to us. It is actually that such things take time and I believe that Namibia is thinking very carefully about how it looks at home and one must understand that. And as I said, I hope that we will come a conclusion soon, but I cannot set a date for it.

What is your objective, the objective of the German side?

That was honestly also my personal objective when I accepted the task. Because I have always been preoccupied with aspects of German history and, admittedly, during the first half of the 20th century, it was very bad. So from the very beginning I found it very worthwhile to work with this part of the German past, which can only be regarded with horror, in such a way as we did with the time from 1933 to 1945 and around the time of the First World War, which we managed to do quite successfully.

And if we look at it and work with it (I had never been to Namibia before and hardly ever even in Africa at all), then we must be deeply shocked about the language, which some 100 years ago was used in Germany about this matter and naturally about the brutality of the rule of German South West Africa. Not just that alone, but that as well.

The objective, just as it was with the talks with Israel, with Jewish organisations, with Poland, with the French and Dutch, is therefore to prove that we see these crimes today in the same way as the victims did then. And that we are sorry. And that of course we cannot undo it, but we can do as much as possible to develop the bilateral relationship and of course, that we will learn from our own behaviour for the future. Naturally, nowadays no one is tempted to acquire colonies any more, but for in dealing with people of different colour there is no doubt that we have much to learn, even nowadays.

Also, whether this succeeds depends on many factors, mainly whether there will be groups in Namibia, such as the Polish bishops who wrote a letter in the 60s, who show that they are ready for reconciliation. This can happen differently today, and I do have the impression that in particular the Namibian Church is thinking in this direction. But we have to wait and simply hope that this process will start. If it takes more time, we must understand that. We have no entitlement to reconciliation.

What is the Federal Government and you as their representative, doing differently during these negotiations compared with development aid attempts since 1990?

It is true that Germany has developed a very close relationship with Namibia since its independence, very much in the light of 'this used to be a German colony'. The aid given to Namibia is the most per capita in Sub-Saharan Africa, overall, I believe now close to a billion euros. And I am sure that it was prompted by the feeling that 'not everything went well', so to speak. But there was never an honest connection with this. Perhaps it was not truly admitted, but instead the thinking was 'there we have another country gaining independence; that is very familiar to us', and just as France and Great Britain still have special relationships with their former colonies, at least from the German point of view, we could have the same. This way of thinking may have played a role, I can only guess. In any case, it was never openly expressed that we got so deeply involved because there had been a genocide in the past.

Neither was it easy to find the language and type of organisation to establish this connection. Because of the reparation claims of other countries – remember what we will have to discuss with Poland and possibly with Russia because of Leningrad, as well as with Greece – the Department of International Law always attaches great importance to keeping a safe distance from the legal issue. I am a lawyer myself, so that is understandable because it's possible to reduce a question down to its legal components, such as a legal acknowledgement of guilt. Then this recognition is the legal basis and not at all what happened in the past.

Therefore, we must take great care that the political and moral core of this connection is made very clear, that it is not misunderstood and seem as if this was all about reparations in the legal sense. It is important for all that something happens, and yes, something will happen.

What above all would you like to see fulfilled?

My task will be complete when the German and the Namibian side sign a resolution; we have not discussed these issues in detail, but if I could achieve a symbolic handshake, my mandate would be fulfilled. This includes a declaration of an order by both parliaments, the German and the Namibian, which would be the basis for further steps. And as already said, the plea for forgiveness. I cannot yet say who will deliver this, the Chancellor or the Federal President. After all, it was Mr Steinmeier who appointed me to conduct the negotiations, he has a particular interest in them and keeps an eye on them. I had a talk with him, and he is willing. I also had a lengthy discussion with Ms Merkel about this matter. She too is very interested in the process and open to an apology for the genocide. But we still have to work out in what form, with which gestures and on what occasion. And a plea for forgiveness, in whatever form or wording, even spontaneous, whether one adds one's own words to the manuscript or omits some – it can only be part of it. The validity is proved by agreements for the future. And above all: the gesture has to be culturally comprehensible in both countries.

Would the year 2020, the 30th anniversary of Namibia's independence, be a suitable benchmark?

With regards to timing, we have a rather different limit to our negotiations. In November there will be general elections in Namibia. It would be nice to conclude the negotiations before that, but I cannot possibly predict this. We would rather not wait until 2020. But I do not wish to speculate further about timing. Another thing that makes it difficult for me is that normally I am used to fixed dates for negotiation sessions. But in this case, we are going from session to session without a fixed end date and it is difficult to plan ahead. That can be difficult. I am retired, have other obligations and this is an honorary position. However, this is just something we have to accept.

Do you actually have a budget for the negotiations?

I am not able to talk about that. It is not easy, anyway, since the Treasury and the Foreign Office and also the Ministry of Economic Cooperation and Development will have to cooperate. That does not always happen without friction. Of course, we have a scale, and of course it is about money that is supposed to mainly benefit the Herero and Nama, since they are the victims. But if we build a hospital or a technical college, all people can use it, and that too is important for a successful domestic future in Namibia.

Do you feel that the negotiations threaten a peaceful coexistence of the Namibians, in particular between the black and white populations?

I wouldn't say so. During my stays in Namibia I also visited the Namibian international school. The class I visited consisted of mainly white students. But that was a coincidence. I then asked whether they also had friends outside their community and thought initially no one will put their hands up, but all of them went up. And as we walked across the playground the head teacher addressed each child by name. The school consists of 1000 students and she knew them all. When asked about it, she explained that she wants all of them to feel welcome and be part of the school community.

To what extent is land reform part of the negotiations?

Land reform in Namibia is indeed part of the discussions between Windhoek and Berlin. But you have to look at this locally. Of course, first you think farms of more than 40,000 hectares, how can that be possible? Here in North Rhine-Westphalia it would be massive. But if you look on the ground there is so much thorny thicket, almost like a fenced desert. And you need that size in order to get any sort of yield. The Namibian government is nevertheless trying to re-distribute the land, but during independence the country gave itself a new constitution, consciously protecting property, in contrast to Zimbabwe, which saw forced expropriations. Today the Namibian government offers to buy land from farmers. But this only works on the principle: 'willing seller, willing buyer'. Indirectly, Germany supports this by providing money.

You may ask why it is so important to protect property in Namibia. The answer is, tourism is a hugely important source of income. If they did not feel safe, tourists would no longer visit. And Germany is not able to support legal processes which would lead to expropriation.

Listening to you, I have great hopes – why did it take so long before now?

I think, after the Second World War we have been preoccupied with our own history for a long time. And also, Namibia was then under South African rule. The clock for reappraisal has therefore been ticking for less than thirty years. The years from 1990 onwards were fateful for both countries. We could have tackled the subject a good ten or fifteen years earlier. Yes, that would have been preferable, but we are where we are now and can only work towards sorting things out together.

What kind of support would you like to see for the negotiations?

I would like see patience for the process of the negotiations. We just need to understand that these things take time. I have great hope that the groups of victims, who were not asked by the Namibian government to join the negotiations, will evaluate the results with openness and without prejudice. Because the large projects that have been planned as part of the negotiation process can only be realised with the help of the Namibian government.

Mr Polenz, I thank you for this conversation.

3 Maps

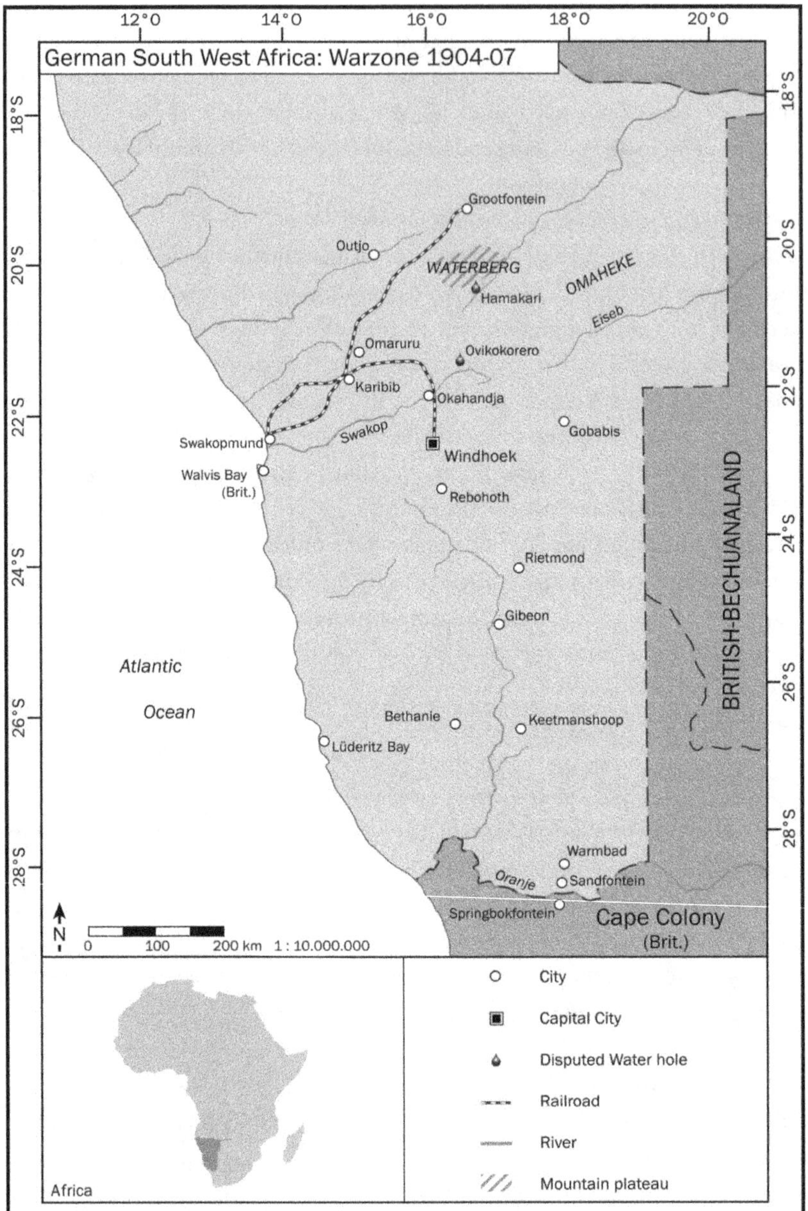

MAP 1 War zone in German South West Africa
REPRINT FROM SUSANNE KUSS, DEUTSCHES MILITÄR AUF KOLONIALEN KRIEGSSCHAUPLÄTZEN: ESKALATION VON GEWALT ZU BEGINN DES 20. JAHRHUNDERTS (2ND EDN, LINKS 2010) 79

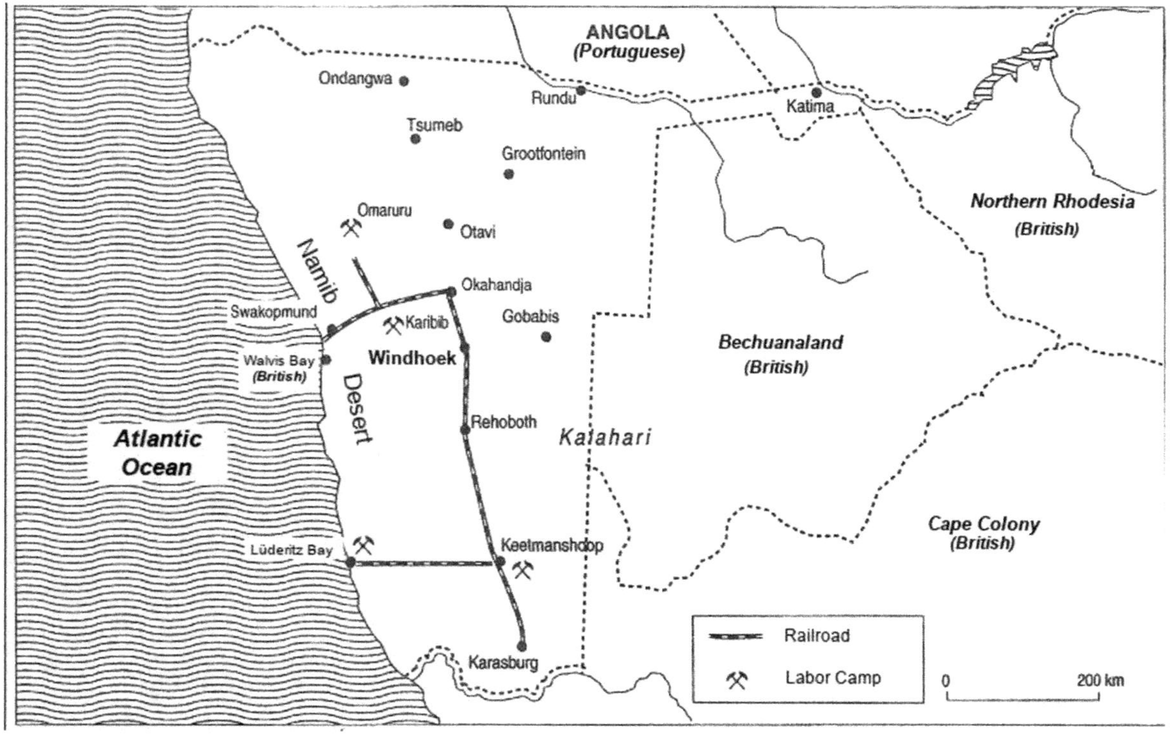

MAP 2 Labour camps in the colony of German South West Africa
REPRINT FROM JOËL KOTEK UND PIERRE RIGOULOT, *DAS JAHRHUNDERT DER LAGER: GEFANGENSCHAFT, ZWANGSARBEIT, VERNICHTUNG* (PROPYLÄEN 2001) 74

4 Register of Persons

All persons mentioned in the main body of the paper are listed here.

Behrendt, Dirk (1971–): German politician (Alliance 90/The Greens), Justice Senator of the State of Berlin since 2016.

Bismarck, Otto von (1815–1898): German politician and statesman, 1871–1890 Chancellor of the Empire; although he first refused to get involved with colonies, he later supported to take over so-called 'protection zones' in Africa, Cameroon, Togo and on the pacific islands.

Brandt, Willy (1913–1992): German Politician (SPD), 1969–1974 German Chancellor as head of a social democratic/liberal coalition, known for his symbolic genuflection on 7th December 1970 in Warsaw at the monument for the dead in the ghetto of Warsaw.

Brosda, Carsten (1974–): German politician (SPD), Senator of the Hamburg Authority for Culture and Media since 2017.

Bülow, Bernhard von (1849–1929): German politician and statesman, justified German colonial interests in 1897 by saying: 'we do not wish to overshadow anyone, but we also demand our place in the sun',[363] 1900–1909 Chancellor of the Empire.

Deimling, Berthold von (1853–1944): German Officer, leader in German South West Africa from 1904, 1906/07 Commandant and nomination for General Major in the first world war in Alsace and Flanders, he then took up a pacifist position.

Eid, Ursula (1949–): German politician (Alliance 90/The Greens), 1998–2005 parliamentary secretary of state as Minister for Economic Cooperation and Foreign Aid, 2001–2005 Chancellor's G8 representative for Africa.

Engert, Stefan (1972–): German political scientist, 2008–2010 research project 'Entschuldigung und Versöhnung in der internationalen Politik' at the Ludwig-Maximilian University Munich, sponsored by the Deutsche Stiftung Friedensforschung (peace research grant).

Erdogan, Recep Tayyip (1954–): Turkish politician (conservative AKP), 2003–2014 Prime Minister of Turkey; directly elected State President of the Turkish Republic since the 2014 change of the system to a presidential system. To his opponents he is an autocrat.

Estorff, Ludwig von (1859–1943): German Officer (General), from 1894 in German South West Africa, then in German East Africa, 1904–07 participation in the German-Namibian war; 1907 – 11 Commander in the colony, then the First World War at the Western Front, later participating in the Kapp Putsch.

363 He coined the expression for 'Weltmachtstreben' (striving for world power) in 1897, Stenographic reports about the negotiations of the Reichstag (Parliament), 6 December 1897, IX. Parliamentary period, V. session, vol 1, 1897/98, 60/B, Bernhard von Bülow.

Fein, Helen (1943–): American social scientist; expert in comparative genocide research; founder of the International Association of Genocide Scholars (IAGS).

Fischer, Joschka (Joseph) (1948–): German politician (Alliance 90/The Greens); 1998–2005 Minister for Foreign Affairs and Vice Chancellor of the Federal Republic of Germany.

Geingob, Hage (1941–): Namibian politician belonging to the Damara (SWAPO), President of Namibia since 21st March 2015.

Gysi, Gregor Florian (1848–): German lawyer and politician (SED, PDS, Left party), 1990–1998 and member of the German Parliament since 2005.

Herzog, Roman (1934–2017): German lawyer and politician (CDU), 1994–1999 Federal President of Germany, visited Namibia 4th – 8th March 1998.

Joseph Frederiks II. (?–1893): Nama name: !Khorebeb-||Naixab, Captain of the OrlamNama, party in the land sale to Adolf Lüderitz, where he assumed to be selling a much smaller area of land than actually came to pass ('Meilenschwindel' or 'mile trick'); his complaint to the Imperial Government remained unanswered.

Lammert, Norbert (1948–): German politician (CDU), 1980–2017 member of the German Parliament; from 2002 Vice President and from 2005 to 2017 President of the German Parliament.

Lemkin, Raphael (1900–1959): Polish-Jewish lawyer and peace researcher; he lost large numbers of his family in the Holocaust; he coined the term 'genocide' and from 1947 worked for the United Nations on a draft law for the punishment of genocides.

Leutwein, Theodor von (1849–1921): German Officer (major general), from 1893 in German South East Africa, 1895–1904 Commander of the protective force and Governor; installing an indirect rule of hegemony; 1904 return to Germany, 1905 retirement.

Lüderitz, Franz Adolf Eduard von (1834–1896): Bremen tobacco wholesaler, acquired on 1st May 1883 the bay of Angra Pequena from Nama Captain Joseph Frederiks II, without defining the type of miles (German/English); demanded protection for this from Bismarck.

Kohl, Helmut (1930–2017): German politician (CDU), 1982–1998; sixth German Chancellor of the Federal Republic of Germany in a CDU/CSU/FDP coalition.

Macron, Emmanuel (1977–): French politician, President of State of France since 1917; he announced a cultural political change of direction regarding the handling of disputed cultural goods at a speech in Burkina Faso.

Maharero, Samuel (1865–1923): Herero Chief in the region of Okahandja; from 1890 onwards Head Chief; first German alliance partner, then opponent; 1904 flight to Bechuanaland (today Botswana), where he died; transferred to Okahandja; a culturally important funeral.

Merkel, Angela (1954–): German politician (CDU), German Chancellor since 2005 in various coalitions.

Movassat, Niema (1984–): German politician (Left party), Member of German Parliament since 2009, member of the Committee for Economic Cooperation and Foreign Aid.

Müntefering, Michelle (1980–): German journalist and politician (SPD), Minister for Foreign Cultural and Educational Policy since March 2018.

Ngavirue, Zedekia Josef (Zed) (1933–): Namibian scientist of Herero origin and ambassador for many years at the European Union and in European countries; special envoy of the Namibian government in the negotiations with Germany.

Nujoma, Samuel Daniel Shafiishuna, (Sam) (1929–): Namibian politician from the Ovamboland people (Ovamboland People's Organisation, SWAPO), from 1990 to 2005 President of the Namibian Republic.

Özdemir, Cem (1965–): German politician (Alliance 90/The Greens), 1994–2002 and since 2013 Member of the German Parliament; from 2004 to 2009 in the European Parliament.

Pieper, Cornelia (1959–): German politician (FDP), Foreign Secretary 2009–2013.

Polenz, Ruprecht (1946–): German politician (CDU), 2005–2013 Chair of the Foreign relations committee of the German Parliament. Special Envoy of the Federal Government concerning the negotiations with Namibia since 4 November 2015.

Reventlow, Ludwig von (1864–1906): German lawyer and politician (Deutschsoziale Partei), Landowner, 1903–1906 Member of the Reichstag Parliament.

Riruako, Kuaima Isaac (1935–2014): Namibian politician, Paramount Chief of the Herero from 1978, initially supporting reparations, since 2001 claimant of the 'Herero People's Reparation Corporation' in the USA to raise legal claims.

Rukoro, Vekuii Reinhard (1954–): Namibian businessman, since 2014 Paramount Chief, head of all Herero, yet not accepted by all of them; after the death of Riruako, he was chief claimant in all legal procedures; he was not part of the German/Namibian negotiations.

Schlieffen, Alfred von (1833–1913): German Field Marshall, Chief of the general staff, author of the strategical operational Schlieffen plan.

Schröder, Gerhard (1944–): German politician (SPD), from 1998 to 2005 Chancellor of the Federal Republic of Germany.

Steinmeier, Frank-Walter (1956–): German politician (SPD); 2005 to 2009 Minister for Foreign Affairs, 2009 to 2013 leader of the opposition; from 2013 to 2017 Foreign Minister; since 2017 President of the Federal Republic of Germany.

Ströbele, Hans-Christian (1939–): German lawyer and politician (Alliance 90/The Greens), from 1998 to 2017 Member of Parliament.

Thierse, Wolfgang (1943–): German politician (SPD), from 1998 to 2005 President of the German Parliament, from 2005 to 2013 its Vice President.

Tjiseseta, Michael (1872–1924): Son of Manasse Tjiseseta, Chief of the Herero in Omaruru.

Trotha, Lothar von (1848–1920): German General, served from 1894–97 as Lieutenant General in German East Africa; 1900/01 in China; from May 1904 as Lieutenant General of the forces in German South West Africa; Proclamation to the Herero people on 2nd October 1904 (known as 'termination order'); 1905 recall.

Trotha, Wolf von and *Trotha, Ulrich*: Still living, distant relatives of General Lothar von Trotha; 2007 journey by several members of the family to Namibia.

Wieczorek-Zeul, H (1942–): German politician (SPD) 1998–2009; German Minister for Economic Cooperation and Development; travelled to Namibia in August 2004 on the occasion the 100-year commemoration of the start of the war.

Wilhelm II (1859–1941): Friedrich Wilhelm Viktor Albert von Preußen, 1888–1918 last German Emperor and King of Prussia; driver of an imperialistic colonial policy.

Zimmerer J (1965–): German global historian and specialist in African Studies, head of the research centre 'Hamburgs (post-)koloniales Erbe/Hamburg und die frühe Globalisierung' since 2014; focus on genocide research.

5 List of Abbreviations

AfD	*Alternative für Deutschland (German political party)*
ATS	*Alien Tort Statute*
BRD	*Bundesrepublik Deutschland (Federal Republic of Germany)*
BT	*Bundestag (German House of Representatives)*
CDU	*Christlich Demokratische Union Deutschlands (German political party)*
CPPCG	*Convention on the Prevention and Punishment of the Crime of Genocide, Deutsch; UN Genocide Convention*
DDR	*Deutsche Demokratische Republik (German Democratic Republic)*
FDP	*Freie Demokratische Partei (German political party)*
G8	*The Group of Eight, supranational association of seven major industrialised nations (G7) and Russia (1998–2004)*
HDI	*Human Development Index*
HPRC	*Herero People's Reparations Corporation*
IGH	*Internationaler Gerichtshof (International Court of Justice), The Hague*
IHDI	*Inequality-adjusted Human Development Index*
nn	*Author not named, in particular with media contributions*
SED	*Sozialistische Einheitspartei Deutschlands (national party of the GDR)*
SPD	*Sozialdemokratische Partei Deutschlands (German political party)*
SWAPO	*South-West Africa People's Organisation (Namibian political party)*
UN	*United Nations*

UNDP *United Nations Development Programme*
VStGB *Völkerstrafgesetzbuch (International Criminal Code)*

6 About the Author

Julia Böcker is a historian, mediator and peace researcher. She has been interested in genocide research since her Master's studies in modern and contemporary history, media studies and public law with a focus on international law in Freiburg (Breisgau), Basel (Switzerland) and Jerusalem (Israel). For several years, she provided practical assistance in court-assisted conflict resolution proceedings in district courts in the USA. In 2019, she completed an additional Master's degree in peace research and security policy at the University of Hamburg with this thesis. Today, she works at the Center for Ethical Education in the Armed Forces (zebis) and lives with her family, including her three children, in Hamburg.

Sources and Literature

Historical Sources

Anz W, 'Gerechtigkeit für die Deutschen in Südwestafrika!' *Die christliche Welt* (Marburg, 7 July 2004).

Behnen M, (ed), *Quellen zur deutschen Außenpolitik im Zeitalter des Imperialismus 1890–1911* (Wissenschaftliche Buchgesellschaft 1977).

Bülow B von, *Denkwürdigkeiten, Band 2, Von der Marokkokrise bis zum Abschied* (Ullstein Verlag 1930).

Estorff L von, *Wanderungen in Südwestafrika, Ostafrika und Südafrika 1894–1910* (Meinert 1979).

Irle J, *Die Herero: Ein Beitrag zur Landes-, Volks-und Missionskunde* (Verlag C. Bertelsmann 1906).

Irle J, *Was soll aus den Herero werden?* (Verlag C. Bertelsmann 1905).

Kommando der Schutztruppen im Reichs-Kolonialamt, Sanitätsbericht über die Kaiserliche Schutztruppe für Südwestafrika, Band 1: Administrativer Teil, Mittler 1909; 8 sowie Band 2: Statistischer Teil, Mittler 1920.

Leutwein T von, Elf Jahre Gouverneur in Deutsch-Südwestafrika (Mittler 1906); *digital collection German Colonialism of the State and University Library Bremen* <http://brema.suub.uni-bremen.de/dsdk/content/titleinfo/1870923>.

Preußen Großer Generalstab, *Die Kämpfe der deutschen Truppen in Südwestafrika auf Grund amtlichen Materials bearbeitet von der Kriegsgeschichtlichen Abteilung I des Großen Generalstabs*, Band 1: Der Feldzug gegen die Herero, Mittler 1906–1908.

Rust C, *Krieg und Frieden im Hererolande: Aufzeichnungen aus dem Kriegsjahre 1904* (Kittler 1905).

Stenographic reports about the negotiations of the Reichstag (Parliament), IX. Parliamentary period, V. session, vol 1, 1897/98, <http://daten.digitale-sammlungen.de/bsb00002771/image_112>.

Stenographic reports about the negotiations of the Reichstag (Parliament) XI. Parliamentary period, LX. session, vol 199, 1903/05, <http://daten.digitale-sammlungen.de/bsb00002809/image_138>.

Stenographic reports about the negotiations of the Reichstag (Parliament), XI. Parliamentary period, V. session, vol. 214, 1906, <http://www.reichstagsprotokolle.de/Blatt_k11_bsb00002824_00102.html>.

Techow J, Telegram to the Foreign Office, Berlin (11 January 1904), Federal Archive (Germany), location Berlin-Lichterfelde, inventory Imperial Colonial Office, R 1001/2111 <https://weimar.bundesarchiv.de/DE/Content/Virtuelle-Ausstellungen/Der-Krieg-Gegen-Die-Herero-1904/der-krieg-gegen-die-herero-1904.html>1.

Trotha L von, Proclamation to the Herero people, 2 October 1904, in: M Behnen (ed), *Quellen zur deutschen Außenpolitik im Zeitalter des Imperialismus 1890–1911* (Wissenschaftliche Buchgesellschaft 1977) 291.

Vedder H, *Kurze Geschichten aus einem langen Leben* (Verlag der Rheinischen Missionsgesellschaften 1953).

Ziegler H, 'Erinnerungen aus dem Herero-Aufstande' (1906) 42 *Daheim* 11.

Sources with Legal References

(Geneva) Convention (22 August 1864) for the Amelioration of the Condition of the Wounded and Sick in Armed Forces in the Field, in: B Wagner (ed), Archiv des Humanitären Völkerrechts in bewaffneten Konflikten, Band 2/I <http://www.humanitaeres-voelkerrecht.de/HVR.II.1.pdf>176.

Commission for International Law of the United Nations, Draft Articles on Responsibility of States for Internationally Wrongful Acts, UN-Document A/56/10 (2001 / 2008) <https://legal.un.org/ilc/texts/instruments/english/commentaries/9_6_2001.pdf>.

Law on the Accession of the Federal Republic of Germany to the Convention of 9 December 1948 on the Prevention and Punishment of the Crime of Genocide, Federal Law Gazette (Bundesgesetzblatt) part II no. 15, 12 August 1954 729, <https://dejure.org/BGBl/1954/BGBl._II_S._729>.

Ruhashyankiko N (ed), UN-Study of the Question of the Prevention and Punishment of the Crime of Genocide, Dokument E/CN.4/Sub.2/416 (4 July 1978) <https://digitallibrary.un.org/record/663583/files/E_CN.4_Sub.2_416-EN.pdf>.

Convention on the Prevention and Punishment of the Crime of Genocide (CPPCG), Decision by Resolution 260 A (III) of the UN General Assembly on 9 December 9 1948, entry into force on 12 January 1951 <https://treaties.un.org/doc/publication/unts/volume%2078/volume-78-i-1021-english.pdf>.

Code of Crimes against International Law of the Federal Republic of Germany (CCAIL), https://www.gesetze-im-internet.de/vstgb/BJNR225410002.html.

Political Sources

'A new Awakening for Europe. A new Dynamic for Germany. A new Solidarity for our Country', coalition agreement of CDU, CSU and SPD for the 19th election period of the German Federal Parliament (Bundestag) (Berlin, 12 March 2018) <https://www.bundesregierung.de/breg-de/themen/koalitionsvertrag-zwischen-cdu-csu-und-spd-195906>.

Adichie CN, 'Eröffnung der Ausstellungen des Ethnologischen Museums und des Museums für Asiatische Kunst der Staatlichen Museen zu Berlin' (Speech at the ceremony in the Humboldt Forum, Berlin, 22 September 2021) <https://www.humboldtforum.org/de/programm/digitales-angebot/digital/festrede-von-chimamanda-adichie-32872/>.

Foreign Office of Germany, Namibia: Beziehungen zu Deutschland (Berlin, 21 December 2021) https://www.auswaertiges-amt.de/de/aussenpolitik/laender/namibia-node/bilateral/208320.

'Daring more progress'. Coalition agreement between the SPD, Alliance 90/The Greens and the FDP for the 20th legislative period of the German Bundestag (Berlin, 7 December 2021) https://www.bundesregierung.de/breg-de/service/gesetzesvorhaben/koalitionsvertrag-2021-1990800.

German Bundestag, document, 16 June 2004, 15/3329, Commemorating the victims of the colonial war in what was then German South-West Africa (motion by the parliamentary groups of the SPD and Alliance 90/The Greens) <http://dipbt.bundestag.de/dip21/btd/15/033/1503329.pdf>.

German Bundestag, document, 9 March 2007, 16/4649, Recognition and reparation of German colonial crimes in former German South-West Africa (motion by the parliamentary group of the Left Party <http://dipbt.bundestag.de/dip21/btd/16/046/1604649.pdf>.

German Bundestag, plenary protocol, 13 June 2007, 16/102, Recognition and reparation of German colonial crimes in former German South-West Africa <http://dip21.bundestag.de/dip21/btp/16/16102.pdf>.

German Bundestag, document, 23 June 2008, 16/9708, Offer to the Namibian National Assembly for a parliamentary dialogue on the reconciliation issue (motion by the parliamentary groups of Alliance 90/The Greens) <http://dipbt.bundestag.de/dip21/btd/16/097/1609708.pdf>.

German Bundestag, document, 1 July 2015, 18/5385, Strengthening relations between Germany and Namibia and living up to our historical responsibility (motion by the parliamentary group of Alliance 90/The Greens) <http://dipbt.bundestag.de/dip21/btd/18/053/1805385.pdf>.

German Bundestag, document, 1 July 2015, 18/5407, Reconciliation with Namibia – Commemoration of and apology for the genocide in the former colony of German South-West Africa (motion by the parliamentary group of the Left Party) <http://dipbt.bundestag.de/dip21/btd/18/063/1806376.pdf>.

German Bundestag, document, 11 July 2016, 18/9152, Status of the negotiations on the reconciliation process with Namibia and on coming to terms with the genocide against the Herero and Nama, (minor enquiry by the parliamentary group of the Left Party) <http://dip21.bundestag.de/dip21/btd/18/091/1809152.pdf>.

German Bundestag, document, 31 May 2016, 18/8613, Remembrance and commemoration of the genocide of the Armenians and other Christian minorities in 1915 and 1916 (motion by the parliamentary groups of the CDU/CSU, SPD and Alliance 90/The Greens) <https://dip21.bundestag.de/dip21/btd/18/086/1808613.pdf>.

German Bundestag, plenary protocol, 17 June 2004, 15/114, Commemorating the victims of the colonial war in what was then German South-West Africa (debate on the motion by the parliamentary groups of the SPD and Alliance 90/The Greens), 10424B–10429 <http://dip21.bundestag.de/doc/btp/15/15114.pdf>.

German Bundestag, plenary protocol, 22 March 2012, 17/168, Strengthening relations between Germany and Namibia and living up to Germany's historical responsibility (discussion of the motion by the parliamentary groups of the SPD and Alliance 90/The Greens) <http://dipbt.bundestag.de/dip21/btp/17/17168.pdf>.

German Bundestag, plenary protocol, 24 September 2015, 18/124, Reconciliation with Namibia – commemoration of and apology for the genocide in the former colony of German South-West Africa (discussion of the motion by the Left Party) and Strengthening relations between Germany and Namibia and living up to our historic responsibility ((discussion of the motion by the Alliance 90/The Greens) <http://dipbt.bundestag.de/dip21/btp/18/18124.pdf>.

German Bundestag, plenary protocol, 21 March 2019, 19/89, consultation on the recommendation for a decision and the report of the Committee on Economic Cooperation and Development (19th Committee) on the motion by the members of Parliament Helin Evrim Sommer, Niema Movassat, Heike Hänsel, and others and the parliamentary group of the Left Party: Reconciliation with Namibia - Apology and responsibility for the genocide in the former colony of German South-West Africa <http://dip21.bundestag.de/dip21/btp/19/19089.pdf>.

Germany Bundestag – Research and Documentation Services, 'Der Aufstand der Volksgruppen der Herero und Nama in Deutsch-Südwestafrika (1904–1908). Völkerrechtliche Implikationen und haftungsrechtliche Konsequenzen' <https://www.bundestag.de/resource/blob/478060/28786b58a9c7ae7c6ef358b19ee9f1f0/wd-2-112-16-pdf-data.pdf>.

Government press conference (Berlin, 10 July 2015) https://www.bundesregierung.de/breg-<de/aktuelles/pressekonferenzen/regierungspressekonferenz-vom-10-juli-847582>.

Köhler H, former German Federal President, 'Von der Unmöglichkeit, über Afrika zu sprechen' (Speech on the occasion of the Africa Days of the Ministry of Education and Research, Berlin, 18 March 2014) <https://www.horstkoehler.de/reden-texte/von-der-unmoeglichkeit-ueber-afrika-zu-sprechen/>.

Macron E, French President, 'Discours de Ouagadougou' (Speech at the University of Ouagadougou, Burkina Faso, 28 November 2017) <https://www.elysee.fr/emmanuel-macron/2017/11/28/discours-demmanuel-macron-a-luniversite-de-ouagadougou>.

Müntefering M, German Minister of State, 'Rückgabe sterblicher Überreste an Namibia' (Speech at the restitution and commemoration ceremony in the Französische Friedrichsstadtkirche, Berlin, 29 August 2018) <https://www.auswaertiges-amt.de/de/newsroom/muentefering-namibia/2131046>.

Pieper C, German Minister of State, 'Ansprache anlässlich der Feierstunde zur Übergabe von Schädeln namibischen Ursprungs in der Charité' (Speech in the Charité' in Berlin, 30 September 2011) <https://www.auswaertiges-amt.de/de/newsroom/110930-stmpieper-rede-hereronama/247300>.

Steinmeier, F-W, German President, 'Eröffnung der Ausstellungen des Ethnologischen Museums und des Museums für Asiatische Kunst der Staatlichen Museen zu Berlin' (Speech at the ceremony in the Humboldt Forum, Berlin, 22 September 2021) <https://www.humboldtforum.org/de/programm/digitales-angebot/digital/festrede-von-frank-walter-steinmeier-33700/>.

Wieczorek-Zeul H, Federal Minister for Economic Cooperation and Development, 'Zum 100. Jahrestag der Herero-Aufstände' (Speech at the commemorations, Okakarara, Namibia, 14 August 2004) <https://www.dhm.de/archiv/ausstellungen/namibia/rede.pdf>.

Data Sources

Federal Foreign Office, 'Namibia: Beziehungen zu Deutschland' (16 October 2019) <https://www.auswaertiges-amt.de/de/aussenpolitik/laender/namibia-node/bilateral/208320>.

Central Intelligence Agency, 'The World Factbook' (1 November 2023) <https://www.cia.gov/the-world-factbook/countries/namibia>.

United Nations Development Programme (UNDP), 'Human Development Index and its Components' (2019) http://www.hdr.undp.org/en/composite/HDI.

United Nations Development Programme (UNDP), 'Inequalities in Human Development in the 21st Century. Briefing note for countries on the 2019 Human Development Report' (2022) <http://hdr.undp.org/sites/all/themes/hdr_theme/country-notes/NAM.pdf>.

Namibia Statistics Agency, 'Namibia Land Statistics Booklet' (September 2018) <https://nsa.nsa.org.na/wp-content/uploads/2021/09/Namibia_Land_Statistics_2018.pdf>.

Organization for Economic Co-Operation and Development, 'Creditor Reporting System' (2018) <https://stats.oecd.org/Index.aspx?DataSetCode=CRS1>.

Press Releases and Media Contributions

'Bundestagspräsident Lammert nennt Massaker an Herero Völkermord' *Die Zeit* (Hamburg, 8 July 2015).

'Eisenberg feiert trotz Kritik „Mohrenfest"', *Mitteldeutscher Rundfunk* (Erfurt, 22 May 2019).

'Fischer bekennt sich zu deutscher Schuld an Sklaverei' *Süddeutsche Zeitung* (Munich, 3 September 2001).

'Gefährliche Versöhnungsreise' *Süddeutsche Zeitung* (Munich, 7 October 2007).

'German Family's Namibia Apology' *BBC World News* (London, 7 October 2007).

'Look at your own genocide history, President Erdogan tells Germany' Daily Sabah (Istanbul, 5 June 2016).

Bischoff K, 'Justizsenator bittet Opferverbände um Verzeihung' *Berliner Zeitung* (Berlin, 28 August 2019).

Böhmermann J, 'Eier aus Stahl' *Neo Magazin Royal / ZDFneo* (Cologne, 14 November 2019).

Eligon J. 'Colonial Past Weighs on Germany / The Big Hole in Germany's Nazi Reckoning? Its Colonial History' *New York Times* (New York, 11 September 2018) A4.

Fischer S. and Springer M, 'Thierse lobt Namibia' Allgemeine Zeitung (Windhoek, 25 April 2003).

Gesprächsreihe 'Das Humboldt-Forum und seine Geschichte(n)' *Deutschlandfunk*, (Cologne, 2019).

Geyer S, 'Herero-Massaker. Entschuldigung, aber keine Entschädigung' *Frankfurter Rundschau* (Frankfurt, 3 July 2016).

Grill B, 'Aufräumen, aufhängen, niederknallen!', *Die Zeit* (Hamburg, 5 August 2004) 10.

Grütters M and Müntefering M, 'Eine Lücke in unserem Gedächtnis. Gastbeitrag' *Frankfurter Allgemeine Zeitung* (*FAZ*) (Frankfurt, 15 December 2018).

Haarmeyer J, 'Stadt entschuldigt sich bei Herero-und Nama-Opferverbänden' *Hamburger Abendblatt* (Hamburg, 6 April 2018).

Habermalz C, 'Koloniales Nicht-Gedenken in Deutschland' *Deutschlandfunk* (Cologne, 16 February 2018).

Habermalz C, 'Meilenstein im Prozess der Aufarbeitung deutscher kolonialer Schuld' *Deutschlandfunk* (Cologne, 29 August 2019).

Habermalz C, Zaghafte Aufarbeitung nach langer Amnesie *Deutschlandfunk* (Cologne, 5 June 2018).

Habermas R und Lindner U, 'Rückgabe – und mehr!' *Die Zeit* (Hamburg, 13 December 2018).

Heimendahl HD, 'Wir brauchen eine neue Erinnerungskultur' *Deutschlandfunk Kultur* (Berlin, 31 January 2019).

Hintze R-F, 'Die Deutschen haben eine kollektive Verantwortung. Gespräch mit Johann Galtung' *Allgemeine Zeitung* (Windhoek, 10 March 2006).

Jessen H, 'Namibia wartet. Interview mit Andreas Guibeb' (2019), 5 *Politik und Kultur* 4.

Klein S, 'Bitte um Vergebung' *Süddeutsche Zeitung* (Munich, 29 August 2018) 6.

Knoblauch E, 'Aus der Heimat entführt, um Europa zu amüsieren', *Die Zeit* (Hamburg, 6 December 2018) 8.

Knoedler G, 'Umbenennung ist richtiger Schritt. Interview mit Jürgen Zimmerer' *taz, die Tageszeitung* (Berlin, 11 September 2013).

Köckritz A, 'Wie viel darf Versöhnung kosten?' *Die Zeit* (Hamburg, 12 December 2018) 6.

Lammert N, 'Deutsche ohne Gnade' *Die Zeit* (Hamburg, 9 July 2015) 16.

Reuß A, 'Archaische Ansichten' *Süddeutsche Zeitung* (*Munich*, 8 March 2019) 15.

Riecker J, 'Ja, Völkermord' *Die Zeit* (Hamburg, 1 June 2016).

Rieger R, 'Die Säule von Cape Cross geht zurück an Namibia' *Der Tagesspiegel* (Berlin, 18 May 2019) 25.

Ruppel U, 'Wir haben lange Zeit zu viel im Hilfsmodus gedacht. Interview mit Günter Nooke (CDU)' *Berliner Zeitung* (Berlin, 6 October 2018).

Schneider B und Welke O, 'Genozid – Reine Ansichtssache', *Heute Show / ZDF* (Cologne, 3 June 2016).

Schröder A, 'Wir werden kämpfen bis die Gerechtigkeit siegt' *Deutschlandfunk Kultur* (Berlin, 7 April 2018).

Schulze T, 'Reisemuffel und Brückenbauer' *taz, die Tageszeitung* (Berlin, 5 November 2015).

Springer M, 'Eid lehnt Entschädigung ab' Allgemeine Zeitung (Windhoek, 2 May 2003).

Stäcker C, 'Genozid-Debatte in Namibia' *Deutsche Welle* (Berlin / Bonn, 18 March 2022).

Stang M, 'Leichen im Keller – Vom Umgang mit kolonialen Skelettsammlungen' *Deutschlandfunk Kultur* (Berlin, 14 April 2016).

Starzmann P, 'Berliner Justizsenator bittet Herero und Nama um Entschuldigung' *Der Tagesspiegel* (Berlin, 27 August 2019).

Starzmann P, 'Muss das Völkermord-Abkommen mit Namibia neu verhandelt werden? Herero und Nama protestieren gegen Deutschland' *Der Tagesspiegel* (Berlin, 22 September 2021).

Titz C, 'Herr Ziegenfuß ist den Schädel los' *Der Spiegel* (Hamburg 28 August 2018).

Trotier K, 'Das waren in Hamburg geplante Raubzüge', *Die Zeit* (Hamburg, 27 June 2019) 19.

Weidlich B, 'Von Trotha Family Arrives to "Reconcile"' *The Namibian* (Windhoek, 3 October 2007).

Wir sind jetzt am Maximum' *Allgemeine Zeitung* (Windhoek, 30 October 2003).

Zimmerer J, 'Afrika-Beauftragter nicht mehr tragbar!' *Westdeutscher Rundfunk* Cologne, 9 October 2018).

Zimmerer J, 'Erdogan hat einen Nerv getroffen', *Frankfurter Rundschau* (Frankfurt, 24 June 2016).

Additional Internet Sources

'Namibia – Deutschland. Eine geteilte Geschichte'. Exhibition in the Rautenstrauch-Joest-Museum für Völkerkunde Cologne (25 November 2004 to 24 April 2005) <https://www.dhm.de/archiv/ausstellungen/namibia/katalog.htm>.

„Hereroland. Eine deutsch-namibische Geschichte". Thalia Theater Hamburg, world premiere on 19 January 2020 <https://www.thalia-theater.de/stueck/hereroland-2019>.

Ausstellung 'Ovizire. Somgu: From Where Do We Speak? Von Woher Sprechen wir?' Museum am Rothenbaum, Kunst und Kulturen der Welt (MARKK) and art salon M. Bassy in cooperation with the University of Hamburg (Hamburg, 4 December 2018 to 14 April 2019) <https://m-bassy.org/programm/from-where-do-we-speak>.

German Museum Association (Deutscher Museumsbund), 'Guidelines for the Care of Collection from Colonial Contexts' (English version, 2021) <https://www.museumsbund.de/publikationen/guidelines-on-dealing-with-collections-from-colonial-contexts-2/>.

German Protestant Church (Evangelische Kirche in Deutschland, EKD), 'Vergib uns unsere Schuld (Matthäus 6, 12)' EKD-Statement in regard to the genocide in former German South West Africa (24 April 2017) <https://www.ekd.de/ekd_de/ds_doc/erklaerung_voelkermord_deutschsuedwestafrika.pdf>.

Jaspert F, 'Setback for the Descendants of the Nama and Ovaherero Indigenous Peoples' (Völkerrechtsblog, 8 May 2019) <https://voelkerrechtsblog.org/setback-for-the-descendants-of-the-nama-and-ovaherero-indigenous-peoples/>.

Ketzmerick M, 'Postkoloniale Außenpolitik: Wie sich Deutschland in Kamerun engagieren sollte' (PeaceLab-Blog of the Global Public Policy Institute Berlin, 20 May 2019) <https://peacelab.blog/2019/05/postkoloniale-aussenpolitik-wie-sich-deutschland-in-kamerun-engagieren-sollte>.

Kößler R, 'Offene Wunden – Die von Trotha-Familie beim Herero-Gedenktag 2007 in Omaruru (Namibia)' (freiburg-postkolonial.de, 25 October 2007) <http://www.freiburg-postkolonial.de/Seiten/Rez-2007-Koessler-Hererotag.htm>.

Projektverbund Forschungsstelle 'Hamburgs (post-)koloniales Erbe, Hamburg und die frühe Globalisierung' <https://www.kolonialismus.uni-hamburg.de>.

Zeller, 'Andauernde Auseinandersetzungen um das Kolonialkriegerdenkmal in Göttingen – Eine Chronik' (freiburg-postkolonial.de, 1 November 2018) <http://www.freiburg-postkolonial.de/Seiten/Goettingen-kolonialadler.htm>.

Zimmerer J and others, 'In großer Sorge um den Aussöhnungsprozess mit Herero und Nama: Brief an Bundeskanzlerin Angela Merkel' (Hamburg 2 April 2019; open letter published 10 May 2019) <https://www.kolonialismus.uni-hamburg.de/wp-content/uploads/Brief-BKA-und-AA.pdf>.

Zimmerer J, 'Commentary on the publication of the Open Letter' (Hamburg, 10 May 2019) <https://www.kolonialismus.uni-hamburg.de/2019/05/10/offener-brief-an-die-bundesregierung-genozid-an-den-herero-und-nama/>.

Sources of Images

Alexander von Hirschfeld, photograph, Namibia, date unknown (approximately 1905 to 1907), in: Fotografische Sammlung des Museums am Rothenbaum. Kunst und Kulturen der Welt Hamburg (MARKK), Inv.-Nr. 2018.1: 85.

Labour camps in the colony of German South West Africa, reprint from J Kotek and P Rigoulot, *Das Jahrhundert der Lager: Gefangenschaft, Zwangsarbeit, Vernichtung* (Propyläen 2001) 74.

War zone in German South West Africa, reprint from S Kuß, *Deutsches Militär auf kolonialen Kriegsschauplätzen: Eskalation von Gewalt zu Beginn des 20. Jahrhunderts* (2nd edn, Links 2010) 79.

Research Literature

Anderson R J, 'Redressing Colonial Genocide. The Herero's' Cause of Action Against Germany', *in California Law Review 93*, 1055–1090, 2005.

Andrieu K, '"Sorry for the Genocide", How Public Apologies Can Help Promote National Reconciliation', in *Millennium – Journal of International Studies*, 38 (1), 3–23, 2009.

Barth B, *Genozid: Völkermord im 20. Jahrhundert, Geschichte, Theorien, Kontroversen*, München, C.H. Beck, 2006.

Bentley T, 'Empires of Remorse, Narrative, Postcolonialism and Apologies for Colonial Atrocity', *Routledge Series on Global Order Studies*, London, New York, Routledge, 2016.

Berat L, 'Genocide, The Namibian Case against Germany', in *Pace International Law Review 5*, 165–210, 1993.

Berghe, P L van den, 'Race – As Synonym', in Ellis Cashmore (ed), *Dictionary of Race and Ethnic Relations*, 4th edn, London, New York, Routledge, 297, 1996.

Bilder R, 'The Role of Apology in International Law and Diplomacy', in *Virginia Journal of International Law 46* (3), 433–473, 2006.

Bley H, *Kolonialherrschaft und Sozialstruktur in Deutsch-Südwestafrika* 1894–1914, Hamburg, Leibnitz-Verlag, 1968.

Bley H/Schleicher H-G, 'Deutsch-deutsch-namibische Beziehungen von 1960 bis 1990', in Förster, Larissa/Henrichsen, Dag/Bollig, Michael (eds), *Namibia – Deutschland.*

Eine geteilte Geschichte, Widerstand, Gewalt, Erinnerung, Wolfratshausen, ed Minerva, 274–291, 2004.

Böhlke-Itzen J, 'Die bundesdeutsche Diskussion und die Reparationsfrage. Ein "ganz normaler Kolonialkrieg?"', in Melber, Henning (ed), *Genozid und Gedenken. Namibisch-Deutsche Geschichte und Gegenwart*, Frankfurt a. M., Brandes &Apsel, 103–119, 2005.

Brandstetter A-M, 'Provenienz (un)geklärt – und was dann?' Einführung, in Förster, Larissa/Edenheiser, Iris/Fründt, Sarah/Hartmann, Heike (eds), *Provenienzforschung zu ethnografischen Sammlungen der Kolonialzeit, Positionen in der aktuellen Debatte*, Berlin, Arbeitsgruppe Museum der Deutschen Gesellschaft für Sozial- und Kulturanthropologie, 184–191, 2018, <https://edoc.hu-berlin.de/handle/18452/19768> accessed 10 July 2019.

Brehl M, '"Diese Schwarzen haben vor Gott und Menschen den Tod verdient". Der Völkermord an den Herero 1904 und seine zeitgenössische Legitimation', in Wojak, Irmtrud/Meinl, Susanne/Fritz Bauer Institut (eds), *Völkermord und Kriegsverbrechen in der ersten Hälfte des 20. Jahrhunderts*, Frankfurt a. M., Campus-Verlag, 77–97, 2004.

Bridgman J/Worley L J, 'Genocide of the Hereros', in *Totten*, Samuel/Parsos, William S./Charny Israel W. (eds), *Century of Genocide, Eyewitness Accounts and Critical Views*, New York, Routledge, 15–52, 2004, Online-Version, <http://site.ebrary.com/id/10094337> accessed 10 July 2019.

Brumlik M, 'Das Jahrhundert der Extreme', in Wojak, Irmtrud/Meinl, Susanne/Fritz Bauer Institut (eds), *Völkermord und Kriegsverbrechen in der ersten Hälfte des 20. Jahrhunderts*, Frankfurt a. M., Campus-Verlag, 19–36, 2004.

Bürger C, 'Der koloniale Völkermord und die Geschichtspolitik der DDR', *Basler Afrika Bibliographien*, 1, 1–18, 2016.

Carranza R/Correa C/Naughton E, *Reparative Justice. More Than Words, Apologies as a Form of Reparation, International Center for Transitional Justice*, 2015.

Chaumont J-M, *Die Konkurrenz der Opfer, Genozid, Identität und Anerkennung*, Lüneburg, zu Klampen, 2001.

Cooper A D, 'Reparations for the Herero Genocide. Defining the Limits of International Litigation', in *African Affairs 106* (422), 113–126, 2007.

Cunningham M, 'Saying Sorry, The Politics of Apology', in *The Political Quarterly*, 70 (3), 285–293, 2002.

Daase C, 'Addressing Painful Memories. Apologies as a New Practice in International Relations', in Assmann, Aleida/Conrad, Sebastian (eds), *Memory in a Global Age. Discourses, Practices and Trajectories*, Basingstoke, Palgrave Macmillan, 19–31, 2010.

Daase C, 'Entschuldigung und Versöhnung in der internationalen Politik', in *Aus Politik und Zeitgeschichte*, 25–26, 43–49, 2013.

Daase C/Engert S/Renner J, 'Guilt, Apology and Reconciliation in International Relations', in Daase, Christopher/Engert, Stefan (eds), *Apology and Reconciliation in International Relations, The Importance of Being Sorry*, London/New York, Routledge, 1–28, 2016.

Dabag M, 'Genozidforschung, Leitfragen, Kontroversen, Überlieferung', in *Zeitschrift für Genozidforschung*, 1, 6–35, 1999.

Dedering T, 'The German-Herero War of 1904, Revisionism of Genocide or Imaginary Historiography?', in *Journal of Southern African Studies*, 19 (1), 80–88, 1993.

Deutsches Historisches Museum (ed), 2016, *Deutscher Kolonialismus, Fragmente seiner Geschichte und Gegenwart*. Darmstadt, Theiss Verlag.

Drechsler H, *Aufstände in Südwestafrika, Der Kampf der Herero und Nama 1904 bis 1907 gegen die deutsche Kolonialherrschaft*, Berlin, Dietz, 1984.

Drechsler H, *Der Kampf der Herero und Nama gegen den deutschen Imperialismus*, 1884–1915, Berlin, Akademie-Verlag, 1966.

Eckert A, 'Der Kolonialismus im europäischen Gedächtnis', in *Aus Politik und Zeitgeschichte*, 1–2, 31–38, 2008.

Eicker S, *Der Deutsch-Herero-Krieg und das Völkerrecht*, Frankfurt a. M., New York, P. Lang, 2009.

Engert S, 'Das kollektive Gewissen. Warum Staaten sich (nicht) entschuldigen', in Schaede, Stephan/Moos, Thorsten (eds), *Das Gewissen*, Tübingen, Mohr Siebeck, 511–538, 2015.

Engert S, 'Die Staatenwelt nach Canossa. Eine liberale Theorie politischer Entschuldigungen', in *Die Friedens-Warte 86* (1/2), 155–189, 2011.

Engert S, 'Germany – Namibia. The Belated Apology to the Herero', in Daase, Christopher/Engert, Stefan (eds), *Apology and Reconciliation in International Relations, The Importance of Being Sorry*, London, New York, Routledge, 127–145, 2016.

Engert S, 'Politische Schuld, moralische Außenpolitik? Deutschland, Namibia und der lange Schatten der kolonialen Vergangenheit', in Harnisch, Sebastian/Maull, Hans W./Schieder, Siegfried (eds), *Solidarität und internationale Gemeinschaftsbildung*, Frankfurt a. M., Campus Verlag, 2009.

Engert S/Daase C, 'Aufarbeitung von Schuld in den internationalen Beziehungen: Überlegungen zum "erweiterten Schuldbegriff"', Engert, Stefan/Moos, Thorsten (eds), *'Vom Umgang mit Schuld', Eine multidisziplinäre Annäherung*, Frankfurt, Campus Verlag, 347–378, 2016.

Engert S/Jetschke A, 'Transitional Justice 2.0 – Zur konzeptionellen Erweiterung eines noch jungen Forschungsprogramms', *Die Friedens-Warte*, 86 (1/2), 15–43, 2011.

Erichsen C W, 'Zwangsarbeit im Konzentrationslager auf der Haifischinsel', Zimmerer J/Zeller J (eds), *Völkermord in Deutsch-Südwestafrika, Der Kolonialkrieg (1904–1908) in Namibia und seine Folgen*, 3 edn, Bonn, BPB, 64–79, 2016.

Fein H, 'Definition and Discontent' *Labelling, Detecting and Explaining Genocide in the Twentieth Century*, Förster, Stig/Hirschfeld, G (eds), *Genozid in der modernen Geschichte*, Berlin, LIT Verlag, 11–21, 1999.

Fein H, 'Genozid als Staatsverbrechen' *Beispiele aus Ruanda und Bosnien* in Zeitschrift für Genozidforschung, 1, 36–45, 1999.

Fein H, 'Scenarios of Genocide. Models of Genocide and Critical Responses', in Charny, Israel W. (ed), *The Book of the International Conference on Holocaust and Genocide. Volume 1, Towards Understanding, Intervention and Prevention of Genocide*, Boulder, CO, Westview Press, 3–31, 1984.

Felz D, *Das Alien Tort Statute, Rechtsprechung, dogmatische Entwicklung und deutsche Interessen*, Berlin, Duncker & Humblot, 2017.

Gallie W B, Essentially 'Contested Concepts', *Proceedings of the Aristotelian Society*, 56, 167–198, 1956.

Gewald J-B, 'Die Beerdigung von Samuel Maharero und die Reorganisation der Herero', Zimmerer J/Zeller J (eds), *Völkermord in Deutsch-Südwestafrika, Der Kolonialkrieg (1904–1908) in Namibia und seine Folgen*, 3rd edn, Bonn, BPB, 215–225, 2016.

Gewald J-B, 'The Great General of the Kaiser', *Botswana Notes and Records*, 26, 67–76, 1994.

Gewald J-B, 'Towards Redemption', *A Socio-Political History of the Herero of Namibia between 1890 and 1923*, Leiden, CNWGS Publications, 1996.

Gibney M/Roxstrom E, 'The Status of State Apologies' *Human Rights Quarterly*, 23 (4), 991–939, 2001.

Hall S, *Ideologie, Identität, Repräsentation. Ausgewählte Schriften 4,* Hamburg, Argument Verlag, 2004.

Harring S L, 'The Herero Demand for Reparations from Germany', *The Hundred Year Old Legacy of a Colonial War in the Politics of Modern Namibia*, Plessis M du/Peté, S (eds), 'Repairing the Past?' *International Perspectives on Reparations for Gross Human Rights Abuses*, Antwerpen, Intersentia, 437–450, 2007.

Häussler M, 'Der Genozid an den Herero', *Krieg, Emotion und extreme Gewalt in 'Deutsch-Südwestafrika'*, Weilerswist, Velbrück Wissenschaft, 2018.

Häussler M/Trotha T von,[364] 'Brutalisierung von unten'. *Kleiner Krieg, Entgrenzung der Gewalt und Genozid im kolonialen Deutsch-Südwestafrika* Mittelweg 36, 21 (3), 57–89, 2012.

Heinemann P, 'Die deutschen Genozide an den Herero und Nama', *Grenzen der rechtlichen Aufarbeitung*, Der Staat, 55, 461–487, 2016.

364 It could not be clarified, whether the (deceased) sociologist was related to General von Trotha.

Henrichsen D, 'Die Hegemonie der Herero in Zentralnamibia zu Beginn der deutschen Kolonialherrschaft', in Förster, Larissa/Henrichsen, Dag/Bollig, Michael (eds), *Namibia – Deutschland. Eine geteilte Geschichte, Widerstand, Gewalt, Erinnerung*, Wolfratshausen, Ed. Minerva, 44–60, 2004.

Henrichsen D, 'EhirOvaherero', *Mündliche Überlieferungen von Herero zu ihrer Geschichte im vorkolonialen Namibia*, WerkStatt Geschichte, 9, 15–24, 1994.

Henrichsen D, 'Herrschaft und Alltag im vorkolonialen Zentralnamibia', *Das Herero und Damaraland im 19. Jahrhundert*, Basel, Windhoek, Basler Afrika Bibliographien, Namibia Wissenschaftliche Gesellschaft, 2011.

Herman J L, *Trauma and Recovery*, London, Pandora, 2015.

Heyden U van der/Zeller J (eds), *Kolonialismus hierzulande, Eine Spurensuche in Deutschland*, Erfurt, Sutton, 2007.

Hillebrecht W, 'Certain Uncertainties or Venturing Progressively into Colonial Apologetics?', in *Journal of Namibian Studies*, 1, 73–95, 2014.

Hockerts H G, 'Wiedergutmachung in Deutschland 1945–1990. Ein Überblick', in *Aus Politik und Zeitgeschichte*, 25–26, 15–22, 2013.

Honold A, 'Afrikanisches Viertel', *Straßennamen als kolonialer Gedächtnisraum*, Kundrus, B (ed), *Phantasiereiche. Zur Kulturgeschichte des deutschen Kolonialismus*, Frankfurt a. M., Campus, 305–321, 2003.

Hull I V, 'Absolute Destruction', *Military Culture and the Practices of War in Imperial Germany*, Ithaca, Cornell University Press, 2005.

Jaguttis M, 'Koloniales Unrecht im Völkerrecht der Gegenwart', Melber, H (ed), *Genozid und Gedenken. Namibisch-deutsche Geschichte und Gegenwart*, Frankfurt a M., Brandes & Apsel, 121–140, 2005.

Jamfa L, 'Germany Faces Colonial History in Namibia', *A Very Ambiguous 'I Am Sorry'*, Gibney, M/Howard-Hassmann, R E/Coicaud, Jean-Marc/Steiner N (eds), *The Age of Apology, Facing Up to the Past* (Pennsylvania Studies in Human Rights), Philadelphia, University of Pennsylvania Press, 202–215, 2008.

Kämmerer J A, 'Colonialism', *Oxford Public International Law*, <https://opil.ouplaw.com/abstract/10.1093/law:epil/9780199231690/law-9780199231690-e690?rskey=ETRWxi&result=1&prd=OPIL> accessed 10 July 2019.

Kämmerer J A/Föh J, 'Das Völkerrecht als Instrument der Wiedergutmachung?' *Eine kritische Betrachtung am Beispiel des Herero-Aufstandes*, Archiv des Völkerrechts, 42 (3), 294–328, 2004.

Karch D, *'... selbst wenn wir sie dabei auslöschen' Entgrenzte Gewalt in der kolonialen Peripherie, in Jahrbuch für Europäische Überseegeschichte*, 10, 93–119, 2010.

Kietzerow A, 'The Crimes of Past Regimes', *When A State should not Apologise*, 2019. Unpublished manuscript, introduced on the congress of EUROISME, the International Society for Military Ethics in Europe, Vienna, 23/05/2019.

König H/Kohlstruck M/Wöll A (eds), *Vergangenheitsbewältigung am Ende des zwanzigsten Jahrhunderts, Opladen*, Westdeutscher Verlag, 1998.

Kößler R, 'Namibia and Germany', *Negotiating the Past*, Windhoek, Namibia, University of Namibia Press, 2015.

Kößler R/Melber H, 'Völkermord – und was dann?' *Die Politik deutsch-namibischer Vergangenheitsbearbeitung*, Frankfurt a M, Brandes & Apsel, 2017.

Kößler R/Melber H, 'Völkermord und Gedenken'. *Der Genozid an den Herero und Nama 1904–1908*, Wojak, Irmtrud/Meinl, Susanne/Fritz Bauer Institut (eds), Frankfurt a M, Campus-Verlag, 37–76, 2004.

Kotek J/Rigoulot P, 'Das Jahrhundert der Lager', *Gefangenschaft, Zwangsarbeit, Vernichtung*, Berlin, Propyläen, 2001.

Krüger G, 'Bestien und Opfer', *Frauen im Kolonialkrieg*: Zimmerer J/Zeller, J (eds), *Völkermord in Deutsch-Südwestafrika, Der Kolonialkrieg (1904–1908) in Namibia und seine Folgen*, 3rd edn, Bonn, BPB 142–159, 2016.

Krüger G, 'Das Goldene Zeitalter der Viehzüchter', Zimmerer J/Zeller J (eds), 'Völkermord in Deutsch-Südwestafrika', *Der Kolonialkrieg (1904–1908) in Namibia und seine Folgen*, 3rd edn, Bonn, BPB 13–25, 2016.

Krüger G, 'Knochen im Transfer' – *Zur Restitution sterblicher Überreste in historischer Perspektive*, Stoecker, H/Schnalke, T/Winkelmann, A (eds), 'Sammeln, Erforschen, Zurückgeben?' *Menschliche Gebeine aus der Kolonialzeit in akademischen und musealen Sammlungen*, Berlin, Links 477–492, 2013.

Krüger G, 'Kriegsbewältigung und Geschichtsbewusstsein', *Realität, Deutung und Verarbeitung des deutschen Kolonialkriegs in Namibia 1904 bis 1907*, Göttingen, Vandenhoeck & Ruprecht, 1999.

Kundrus B/Strotbek H, 'Genozid'. Grenzen und Möglichkeiten eines Forschungsbegriffs – ein Literaturbericht, in Neue Politische Literatur, 51 (1), 397–423, 2006.

Kuß S, 'Der Herero-Deutsche Krieg und das deutsche Militär', *Kriegsursachen und Kriegsverlauf*, Förster, L/Henrichsen, D/Bollig, M (eds), 'Namibia – Deutschland', *Eine geteilte Geschichte, Widerstand, Gewalt, Erinnerung,* Wolfratshausen, edn Minerva, 62–77, 2004.

Kuß S, 'Deutsches Militär auf kolonialen Kriegsschauplätzen', *Eskalation von Gewalt zu Beginn des 20. Jahrhunderts*, 2nd edn, Berlin, Links, 2010.

Laak D van, 'Der deutsche Kolonialismus und seine Nachwirkungen', *Aus Politik und Zeitgeschichte,* 4, 3–11, 2005.

Lau B, 'Uncertain Certainties'. *The Herero-German War of 1904,* History and Historiography – 4 Essays in Reprint, 39–52, 1995.

Lemkin R, 'Genocide', *American Scholar*, 15, 227–230, 1946.

Lindner U, 'Deutscher Kolonialismus im internationalen Kontext', in Deutsches Historisches Museum (ed), *Deutscher Kolonialismus, Fragmente seiner Geschichte und Gegenwart*, Darmstadt, Theiss Verlag, 16–29, 2016.

Lindner U, Das Kolonialviertel in München-Trudering, in Heyden, Ulrich van der/ Zeller, Joachim (eds), *Kolonialismus hierzulande, Eine Spurensuche in Deutschland*, Erfurt, Sutton, 293–299, 2007.

Löwenheim N, 'A Haunted Past, Requesting Forgiveness for Wrongdoing in International Relations', in *Review of International Studies*, 35, 531–555, 2009.

Lundtofte H, '"I Believe that the Nation as such must be Annihilated ..." The Radicalisation of the German Suppression of the Herero Rising in 1904', in Jensen, Steven L. B. (eds), *Genocide, Cases, Comparisons and Contemporary Debates, Copenhagen*, Danish Centre for Holocaust and Genocide Studies, 15–53, 2003.

Marrus M R, 'Official Apologies and the Quest for Historical Justice', in *Journal of Human Rights*, 6 (1), 75–105, 2007.

Melber H, '"Wir haben überhaupt nicht über Reparationen gesprochen". Die namibisch-deutschen Beziehungen, Verdrängung oder Versöhnung?', in Zimmerer J/Zeller J (eds), *Völkermord in Deutsch-Südwestafrika, Der Kolonialkrieg (1904–1908) in Namibia und seine Folgen*, 3rd ed, Bonn, BPB, 215–225, 2016.

Melber H, 'Grenzen des (post-)kolonialen Staates, Von Deutsch-Südwest nach Namibia', in Becker, Joachim/Komlosy, Andrea (eds), *Grenzen Weltweit. Zonen, Linien Mauern im historischen Vergleich*, 2nd ed, Vienna, Promedia-Verlag, 125–140, 2006.

Mihai M, 'When the State Says "Sorry"', *State Apologies as Exemplary Political Judgments*, The Journal of Political Philosophy, 21 (2), 200–220, 2013.

Minow M, *Between Vengeance and Forgiveness, Facing History after Genocide and Mass Violence*, reprint, Boston, Beacon Press, 2009.

Moses D, Raphael Lemkin, 'Culture and the Concept of Genocide' Bloxham, D/Moses, D A (eds), *The Oxford Handbook of Genocide Studies*, Oxford, New York, Oxford University Press, 19–41, 2010.

Negash G, 'Apologia Politica', *States & their Apologies by Proxy*, Lanham, MD, Lexington Books, 2006.

Nobles M, *The Politics of Official Apologies*, New York, Cambridge University Press, 2008.

Nuhn W, 'Sturm über Südwest'. *Der Hereroaufstand von 1904, Ein düsteres Kapitel der deutschen kolonialen Vergangenheit Namibias*, Koblenz, Bernard & Graefe, 1989.

Paech N, 'Der juristische Weg der Wiedergutmachung', *Schadensersatz für Völkermord?*, in Böhlke-Itzen, J (ed), *Kolonialschuld und Entschädigung. Der deutsche Völkermord an den Herero 1904–1907*, Frankfurt a M, Brandes & Apsel, 11–26, 2004.

Poewe K, 'The Namibian Herero', *A History of their psychosocial disintegration and survival, Lewiston* et al, Mellen Press, 1985.

Pool G, *Samuel Maharero*, Windhoek, Namibia, Gamsberg Macmillan, 1991.

Quigley J, 'Intent Without Intent', Jones A (ed), *Genocide in Theory and Law*, London, Sage 86–94, 2008.

Ratner S R./Abrams J S/Bischoff J, *Accountability for Human Rights Atrocities in International Law, Beyond the Nuremberg Legacy*, 3rd edn, Oxford, New York, Oxford University Press, 2009.

Robel Y, 'Verhandlungssache Genozid', *Zur Dynamik geschichtspolitischer Deutungskämpfe*, München, Fink, 2013.

Roos U/Seidl T, 'Im "Südwesten" nichts Neues? Eine Analyse der deutschen Namibiapolitik als Beitrag zur Rekonstruktion der außenpolitischen Identität des deutschen Nationalstaates', *Zeitschrift für Friedens-und Konfliktforschung*, 4 (2), 182–224, 2015.

Said E W, *Orientalism*, New York, Pantheon Books, 1978.

Sarkin J, 'Germany's Genocide of the Herero', *Kaiser Wilhelm II, his General, his Settlers, his Soldiers*, Cape Town, South Africa et al, James Currey, 2010.

Schabas W A, 'The Law and Genocide', Bloxham, D/Moses, Dirk A (eds), *The Oxford Handbook of Genocide Studies*, Oxford, New York, Oxford University Press, 123–141, 2010.

Schabas W/Fliessbach H, *Genozid im Völkerrecht*, Hamburg, Hamburger edition, 2003.

Schaller D J, 'Genocide and Mass Violence in the "Heart of Darkness"', *Africa in the Colonial Period*, Bloxham, D/Moses, D A (eds), The Oxford Handbook of Genocide Studies, Oxford, New York, Oxford University Press, 345–364, 2010.

Schaller D J, 'Genozidforschung', *Begriffe und Debatten*, Schaller, D J/Boyadjian, R/Berg, V/Scholtz, H (eds), Zürich, Chronos-Verlag 9–26, 2004.

Schwarzer A, 'Nama und Herero', *Völkermord ohne Entschädigung? Blätter für deutsche und internationale Politik*, 60, 13–16, 2015.

Seibert-Fohr A, United States Alien Tort Statute, in Oxford Public International Law, 2015, <https://opil.ouplaw.com/view/10.1093/law:epil/9780199231690/law-9780199231690-e743> accessed 10/09/2019.

Sobich F O, 'Schwarze Bestien, rote Gefahr', *Rassismus und Antisozialismus im deutschen Kaiserreich*, Frankfurt a M, Campus, 2006.

Speitkamp W, 'Kolonialdenkmäler', in Zimmerer J (ed), *Kein Platz an der Sonne. Erinnerungsorte der deutschen Kolonialgeschichte*, Bonn, BPB, 409–423, 2013.

Stoler A L, 'Colonial Aphasia', *Race and Disabled Histories in France*, Public History 23 (1), 121–156, 2011.

Strübbe K, 'Politische Entschuldigungen', *Theorie und Empirie des sprachlichen Handelns*, Wiesbaden, Springer VS, 2018.

Sudholt G, *Die deutsche Eingeborenenpolitik. Von den Anfängen bis 1904. Hildesheim*, Olms, 1975.

Tavuchis N, 'Mea Culpa', *A Sociology of Apology and Reconciliation*, Stanford, Kalifornien, Stanford University Press, 1991.

Tetzlaff R, 'Afrika', *Eine Einführung in Geschichte, Politik und Gesellschaft*, Wiesbaden, Springer VS, 2018.

Thompson J, 'Apology, Justice and Respect', *A Critical Defence of Political Apology*, Gibney, M/Howard-Hassmann, Rhoda E/Coicaud, J-M/Steiner, N (eds), 'The Age of Apology', *Facing Up to the Past* (Pennsylvania Studies in Human Rights), Philadelphia, University of Pennsylvania Press, 31–44, 2005.

Thompson J, 'Is a Sorry Affair', *Social & Legal Studies 21* (2), 215–225, 2012.

Thompson J, 'Taking Responsibility for the Past', *Reparation and Historical Injustice*, Cambridge et all, Polity Press, 2002.

Trotha T von, 'Genozidaler Pazifierungskrieg'. *Soziologische Anmerkungen zum Konzept des Genozids am Beispiel des Kolonialkriegs in Deutsch-Südwestafrika*, Zeitschrift für Genozidforschung, 4, 30–57, 2003.

Verhoeven J, 'Le Crime de Génocide', *Originalité et Ambiguïté*, Revue Belge de Droit International, 1, 5–26, 1991.

Walter D, 'Kein Pardon'. *Zum Problem der Kapitulation im Imperialkrieg*, Mittelweg 36, 21 (3), 90–111, 2012.

Watts A, 'The Art of Apology', Ragazzi, M (ed), *International Responsibility Today*, Essays, Leiden, Boston, Martin Nijhoff, 107–116v, 2005.

Weyeneth R, 'The Power of Apology and the Process of Historical Reconciliation', *The Public Historian* 23 (3) 9–38, 2001.

Wieczorek-Zeul H, 'In the Words of the Lord's Prayer'. *Bitte um Vergebung für die Verbrechen an den Nama und Herero*, Welt bewegen, Erfahrungen und Begegnungen, Berlin, Vorwärts-Buch, 41–51, 2007.

Wieczorek-Zeul H, Foreword, Kößler, R/Melber, H (eds), *Völkermord – Und was dann? Die Politik deutsch-namibischer Vergangenheitsbearbeitung*, Frankfurt a M, Brandes & Apsel, 9–11, 2017.

Winstel T, 'Vergangenheit verjährt nicht'. *Über Wiedergutmachung*, Aus Politik und Zeitgeschichte, 25–26, 15–22, 2013.

Zeller J, 'Ombepera i koza', *Die Kälte tötet mich. Zur Geschichte des Konzentrationslagers in Swakopmund (1904–1908)*, Zimmerer, J/Zeller, J (eds), 'Völkermord in Deutsch-Südwestafrika', *Der Kolonialkrieg (1904–1908) in Namibia und seine Folgen*, 3rd edn, Bonn, BPB, 64–79, 2016.

Zeller J, 'Zwischen Wilhelmshaven und München', *(Post-)Koloniale Erinnerungskultur in Deutschland*, Heyden, U/ van der Zeller J (eds), *Kolonialismus hierzulande, Eine Spurensuche in Deutschland*, Erfurt, Sutton, 267–274, 2007.

Zentralkomitee der deutschen Katholiken/Hoppe, T, Authentische Erinnerung – Fundament für tragfähige Versöhnung, Renovabis (ed), *Wege zur Versöhnung. Grundlagen für ein tragfähiges Miteinander*, 82–89, 2018.

Zimmerer J, 'Der erste Völkermord des 20. Jahrhunderts'. *Über den schwierigen Umgang mit Deutschlands kolonialem Erbe*, Deutsches Historisches Museum (ed), *Deutscher Kolonialismus, Fragmente seiner Geschichte und Gegenwart*, Darmstadt, Theiss Verlag, 138–145, 2016.

Zimmerer J, 'Deutsche Herrschaft über Afrikaner', *Staatlicher Machtanspruch und Wirklichkeit im kolonialen Namibia*, 2nd edn, Berlin et all, LIT Verlag, 2002.

Zimmerer J, 'Entschädigung für Herero und Nama', Blätter für deutsche und internationale Politik, 6, 658–660, 2005.

Zimmerer J, 'Kolonialer Genozid?' *Vom Nutzen und Nachteil einer historischen Kategorie für eine Globalgeschichte des Völkermords*, Schaller, D J/Boyadjian, R/Berg, V/Scholtz, H (eds), 'Enteignet – vertrieben – ermordet', *Beiträge zur Genozidforschung*, Zürich, Chronos-Verlag, 109–128, 2004.

Zimmerer J, 'Kolonialismus und kollektive Identität', *Erinnerungsorte der deutschen Kolonialgeschichte* (edn.), 'Kein Platz an der Sonne', *Erinnerungsorte der deutschen Kolonialgeschichte*, Bonn, Bundeszentrale für politische Bildung, 9–38, 2013.

Zimmerer J, 'Krieg, KZ und Völkermord in Südwestafrika', Zimmerer J/Zeller, J (eds), *Völkermord in Deutsch-Südwestafrika, Der Kolonialkrieg (1904–1908) in Namibia und seine Folgen*, 3rd edn, Bonn, BPB, 45–63, 2016.

Zimmerer J, 'Kriegsgefangene im Kolonialkrieg'. *Der Krieg gegen die Herero und Nama in Deutsch-Südwestafrika (1904–1907)*, Overmans, R (ed), *In der Hand des Feindes. Kriegsgefangenschaft von der Antike bis zum Zweiten Weltkrieg, Cologne*, Böhlau Verlag, 277–294, 1999.

Zimmerer J, 'Von Windhuk nach Auschwitz?' *Beiträge zum Verhältnis von Kolonialismus und Holocaust*, Berlin a. o., LIT-Verlag, 2011.

Zimmerer J, *Bevölkerungsökonomie, Rassenstaat und Genozid*, Benz, W (ed), 'Vorurteil und Genozid'. *Ideologische Prämissen des Völkermords*, Vienna, Böhlau Verlag, 15–33, 2010.

Zimmerer J/Zeller, J, 'Foreword', the same (eds), *Völkermord in Deutsch-Südwestafrika, Der Kolonialkrieg (1904–1908) in Namibia und seine Folgen*, 3rd edn, Bonn, BPB, 8–10, 2016.

www.ingramcontent.com/pod-product-compliance
Lightning Source LLC
Chambersburg PA
CBHW071225230926
51849CB00001B/30
* 9 7 8 9 0 0 4 6 8 8 1 9 3 *